THE CHURCH THAT DOES NOT FALL

By
Lee Roy Holmes

TEACH Services, Inc.
Brushton, New York

**PRINTED IN
THE UNITED STATES OF AMERICA**

World rights reserved. This book or any portion thereof may not be copied or reproduced in any form or manner whatever, except as provided by law, without the written permission of the publisher, except by a reviewer who may quote brief passages in a review. The author assumes full responsibility for the accuracy of all facts and quotations as cited in this book.

2010 11 12 13 14 · 5 4 3 2 1

Copyright © 2010 Lee Roy Holmes and TEACH Services, Inc.
ISBN-13: 978-1-57258-610-9
ISBN-10: 1-57258-610-9
Library of Congress Control Number: 2009942552

Unless otherwise noted, all Scripture quotations are from the New King James Bible. All italicized words in material quoted from Ellen White indicate the author's emphasis unless otherwise noted.

Published by

TEACH Services, Inc.
www.TEACHServices.com

ACKNOWLEDGEMENTS

I owe everything to the God who found me in a spiritual wasteland and brought me into the fellowship of His church. I was nurtured in that environment from my youth up by Christian parents, friends, teachers, and pastors.

I am grateful to those who took time from their busy lives to read the manuscript and give valuable counsel: Tom Mostert, Bruce Johnston, Harvey Steck, Jim Brackett, Marilyn Morgan, and Joseph Reeves. I am indebted, too, to the members of the congregations that I have had the privilege of serving as pastor who, with grace and patience, have taught me much about how the church works.

I wish to acknowledge the loving support of my dear wife Marjorie, now deceased, whose love and devotion to both her family and church family was a model worthy of emulation.

Lee Roy Holmes

The Church That Does Not Fall

TABLE OF CONTENTS

Acknowledgements .... *iii*
Introduction .... *vii*

Chapter

1	The Church Is God's Idea	1
2	But What Is the Church?	8
3	And Who Are the Remnant?	21
4	Laodicea Is Not a Bad Word	32
5	The Forgotten Angel	42
6	The Apostasy Question	56
7	How to Protest the Wrongs in the Church	71
8	What a United Church Looks Like	82
9	Some Wolves Wear Wool Suits	96
10	Everyone Submits	110
11	The Church and My Salvation	121
12	Was Jesus a Good Church Member?	130
13	The Issue is Worship	138
14	The Church that Does Not Fall	155

The Church That Does Not Fall

INTRODUCTION

Following the close of the Second World War, I was sent to Japan as part of the United States' occupational forces. The first time I rode the train from Yokohama to Tokyo to attend services in the Japanese Adventist church there, I was shocked by the devastation wrought by US aerial bombardment. The great industrial complex that stretched the twenty miles or so between the two cities was a sea of rubble, except for one thing—the smoke stacks. Apparently even direct hits from the B-29s' bombs did not bring them down. Their concrete and steel forms still stood tall and naked against the sky—scarred but standing.

I found in the survival of those old smoke stacks a rather rough metaphor of something else that will be standing when all other human structures have been reduced to rubble—the church of God. "The church may appear as about to fall, but it does not fall. It remains, while the sinners in Zion will be sifted out—the chaff separated from the precious wheat" (*Selected Messages*, bk. 2, p. 380).

This book is largely the product of my reflections on that statement. Where is the church that does not fall? What does it look like? What keeps it from falling? How can I make sure I am firmly embedded in that church—a part of the wheat that remains when the chaff is blown away in the coming storm?

I believe one of the most neglected subjects in the Adventist doctrinal constellation is the doctrine of the church. If the members of most congregations were given a choice of topics for study and discussion, the church might come in close to last. But, when one remembers that the church is one of just two combatants in earth's final war, to have wrong ideas about the church—its identity and role in the coming apocalypse—could be disastrous. The devil has invented many traps and seductions to hinder the Christian from entering the kingdom, and the one that may be taking many wholly unaware is the subtle sophistry that the church is optional or that its role in the believer's salvation is minimal.

I dream of the day when God's people will be revived, reformed, and fully united in serving Him—for the day when the church will appear "fair as the moon, clear as the sun, and terrible as an army with banners" (Song of Solomon 6:10, KJV). In writing this book, it has been my purpose to share that dream.

    Lee Roy Holmes

Chapter One

THE CHURCH IS GOD'S IDEA[1]

"[It is God's] intent that now the manifold wisdom of God might be made known by the church to the principalities and powers in the heavenly places" (Ephesians 3:10).

Human beings inevitably think of the church as something they have created. If there is a divine element, it tends to be obscured by flow charts, financial statements, chain of command, policy books, and all the features of an ordinary business. It may not be as earthy as Wal-Mart, but hardly more heavenly than the Red Cross. When one factors in the frailties of human leadership, with a bit of politicking and posturing for position, it is only natural that some would find it easy to ignore the church, belittle it, or leave it.

But what if the church really is *God's* idea? What if it is indeed something born out of the divine mind, something as sacred as the tabernacle and temple that enshrined the Shekinah glory? What if it is in truth the body of Christ (1 Corinthians 12:27), the church of the living God (Acts 20:28)? What if Jesus really is the Great Church Builder (Matthew 16:18)? The difference that makes is profound. If God created the church, its study puts us on holy ground. We must remove our shoes and carefully consider what He had in mind.

To understand the place of the church in the divine scheme of things, we must take a moment for an overview of salvation history. Only then can we appreciate those qualities that distinguish the church from anything humans might have put together.

There is good reason to believe that the plan of salvation is the greatest evidence of the wisdom of God in the history of the universe. At least as viewed from Planet

1

Earth everything else falls short. The many marvels of nature—the migration of birds, the engineering of an oak, the genetic encoding of the DNA molecule, the birth of a child, even the creation of whole galaxies—pale by comparison. It was the sin crisis that called forth the greatest demonstration ever of the creative genius of the Godhead.

Who can fully appreciate the magnitude of the challenge God faced? One impossibly difficult question follows hard upon another. What provision can He make for the forgiveness of sin without weakening the requirements of His immutable law? How far can He go in making eternal life attractive and the consequences of disobedience repugnant without violating man's freedom of choice? What part will the recipient of salvation himself have to play in order to receive the gift? How can He provide for both reconciliation and restoration? What will be the "rules of engagement" with which Satan will be made to comply?

The solution that God devised—this holy thing called "the plan of salvation"—can be understood in its essentials by a child, but its outer limits cannot be grasped by the brightest angel mind, and is certainly beyond the reach of the most gifted mortal. Paul exclaims, "Oh, the depth of the riches both of the wisdom and knowledge of God! How unsearchable are His judgments and His ways past finding out!" (Romans 11:33).

The centerpiece of that plan, of course, is the life, death, resurrection, and high-priestly ministry of Jesus. It includes the powerful assistance of the Holy Spirit and the angels. In the council room of heaven, Jesus volunteered to take man's fallen nature, be born in Bethlehem, grow up in Nazareth, work as a carpenter, preach the gospel, and heal the sick. He would endure unimaginable insult and abuse, be crucified, resurrected, and ascend back to heaven. There He would mediate His own blood in the heavenly sanctuary and make preparation to return to earth the second time. Those who accept the

The Church is God's Idea

gift of His substitutionary death and cooperate with the Holy Spirit in overcoming sin could be saved eternally. And we shout, "Amazing grace!" If the plan works, the weakest, the most degenerate, the most rebellious of human beings can be restored to perfect harmony with God. The profligate can be made pure, the self-indulgent self-denying, the greedy generous. God can "be just and the justifier of the one who has faith in Jesus" (Rom. 3:26).

But the plan involves risk. Everything is predicated on Jesus' success in resisting the virus of sin Himself. In order for the plan to work, He must be tempted as man but not yield as every man has done. There is the awesome prospect of failure. Omnipotence has other options: Obliterate sinners and even the memory of sin. Create new worlds populated by loyal subjects. Use almighty power to play it safe.

But love must take the risk. "Christ was under no obligation to make this great sacrifice. Voluntarily He pledged Himself to bear the punishment due to the transgressor of His law. *His love was His only obligation*, and without a murmur He endured every pang and welcomed every indignity that was part of the plan of salvation." (*In Heavenly Places*, p. 43).

As a man, Christ engaged the great enemy of both God and man and won the victory. We hear the shout of triumph echoing through the corridors of heaven: "Now salvation, and strength, and the kingdom of our God, and the power of His Christ have come, for the accuser of our brethren, who accused them before our God day and night, has been cast down. . . . Therefore rejoice, O heavens, and you who dwell in them!" (Revelation 12:10-12).

But wait! Here is a perfect plan, something to make the whole watching universe stand on tiptoe, but by what means shall it be communicated to the lost? After Jesus sets it all in motion and returns to heaven, what agency will be given the practical task of advertising the offer? Who will protect the plan from counterfeits, from false saviors, false gospels, from heresies and heretics? Who will nurture the faith of the newborn? Who will shelter the weak and seek after the wayward?

The answer is found in the third chapter of Ephesians where Paul, speaking of "the privilege of proclaiming to the Gentiles the good news of the unfathomable riches of Christ," tells how this "mystery"—the details of the plan of salvation—was to be put into effect. "It was hidden for long ages in God the creator of the universe, in order that now, through the church, the wisdom of God in all its varied forms might be made known to the rulers and authorities in the realms of heaven" (Ephesians 3:8-10, NEB).

Paul uses expressions like "the unsearchable riches of Christ," "the fellowship of the mystery," and "the manifold wisdom of God" (Ephesians 3:8-10) in an attempt to magnify the marvel and complexity of the plan of salvation. But his exuberance does not disconnect him from the practical necessity of providing a conduit for those blessings. At the center of the sin solution, he places the church, making it an integral, inseparable part of that wisdom and plan. The creation of the Christian church is itself one of the greatest evidences of the love and wisdom of God to be found in the entire universe. The plan of salvation does not work outside of, or apart from, the church.

In the Christian church "there is neither Jew nor Greek, there is neither slave nor free, there is neither male nor female; for you are all one in Christ Jesus" (Galatians 3:28). There is no longer an issue of the Jewish privilege or concern about identifying with the physical lineage of Abraham. National origin, economic status, gender, education—all become meaningless with respect to one's personal salvation when placed in the context of this new creation, the church.

The church is God's idea. People not only need the Lord; they need each other. God recognized that man needed a support group, an extended family, a learning center, a social fellowship, a training school, a place of worship—all in one. So God put it all together and called

The Church is God's Idea

it *ekklesia*, which is the Greek word meaning "a calling out," "a place of assembly." Those called out of the world of evil and error would have a place to be called into. Its members, themselves in need of constant renewal, would not be perfect, but having received the love of Jesus into their hearts, they would be ready to welcome the weary and wounded into their fellowship. There the lonely would find friends; the homeless, a place of refuge; the disinherited, a family; the sick, a place of healing.

Man tends to think of the church as local; God's idea is global. Man is inclined to think of the church as something that ministers to him; God created it as a way for man to minister to others. Man invents worship that puts him at the center; true worship puts God at the center. Man wants the church to make him comfortable in his spiritual apathy; God wants it to be spiritually vital and life-changing.

The church encompasses far too much that is foreign to the human; it has to be God's idea. Hundreds of human church experiments have been, and continue to be, tried. New churches come and go like restaurants. They fail because they fall short of capturing the real essence of the church. The church is more than a denominational label and a place to meet; it is the very presence of Christ with His people (Matthew 18:20). It is the presence and headship of Christ (Ephesians 5:23) that infuses the church with a divine dimension, even an element of mystery that defies definition. It is the unity of the believers that proclaims that headship.

There is reason to believe that the church idea was not something God put together at the last minute to meet the terrible emergency created by the entrance of sin. More likely, as long as God and heaven have existed, there has been a church in heaven where its inhabitants assemble for worship. The morning stars singing together and the sons of God shouting for joy (Job 38:7) may describe such a heavenly convocation. Certainly Revelation 19:1 is such a description: "I heard a loud voice of a great multitude in heaven, saying, 'Alleluia! Salvation and glory and honor and power belong to the Lord our God.'"

Ellen White confirms it: "The church of God below is one with the church of God above. Believers on the earth and beings in heaven who have never fallen constitute one church" (*Testimonies for the Church*, vol. 6, p. 366). "From the beginning it has been God's plan that through His church shall be reflected to the world His fullness and His sufficiency. . . . The church is the repository of the riches of the grace of Christ; and through the church will eventually be made manifest, even to 'the principalities and powers in heavenly places,' the final and full display of the love of God" (*The Acts of the Apostles*, p. 9).

No organization on earth antedates the church, and most organizations to some degree mimic it. It is an integral, absolutely essential part of the divine strategy for saving souls. The wisdom of God is superlatively demonstrated in the creation of the church. It is *in the church* that the great controversy between Christ and Satan is to be consummated. The church, marshaled under the blood-red banner of Immanuel, will be led to victory against the hosts of darkness. The gates of hell shall not prevail.

That all sounds wonderful, even exciting, but still, what, exactly, is the church? That's where we're going next.

Discussion Questions:

1. Do you think the church idea was God's best option? Wouldn't it work just as well or better if each person were taught the truth from the Bible by the Holy Spirit and didn't have to gear in with other people and their opinions?
2. If the church is truly a divinely-created institution, why does our focus seem to be so much more on its human leaders than on the leadership of Christ, more on its human failures that its divine providences?
3. Peter speaks of the church as being composed of those who have been "called out of darkness into His

The Church is God's Idea

marvelous light" (1 Peter 2:9). Do you feel that God has shown His love for you by calling you into the fellowship of His church?

Endnotes

1   I found this title in the *Seventh-day Adventist Elder's Handbook*. 1994.

Chapter Two

BUT WHAT IS THE CHURCH?

"Which is the church of the living God, the pillar and ground of the truth" (1 Timothy 3:15).

If a stranger were to stop you on the street and ask directions to the church, how would you answer? In the first place, you would probably feel a twinge of irritation at the ambiguity of the request. *"The* church?" you ask yourself. There are several churches in town. If all he wants is *a* church, no problem. But *the* church raises the possibility of a heavy discussion about which is the true church. And such debate usually puts people in one of two camps—the one defending a particular denomination as the one God favors, the other arguing that God's true church is known only to Him since His people are scattered in all churches and even outside any church.

Our church search is complicated by the fact that few words have a greater variety of meanings than "church." It's like saying "mother" to an audience of five hundred. The listeners do not rifle through an assortment of dictionary meanings; an image of a particular *person* emerges in each mind. Just so, whatever precise or technical definitions we might give "church," each will have difficulty getting past the resident image in the listener's mind.

A study of Bible metaphors for the church can help us understand the church through the varied imagery which they provide. The church as a "body" (Ephesians 2:16) stresses the *unity* of the believers and the functional relationship of each to the whole. The church as a "bride" (2 Corinthians 11:2) emphasizes *intimacy* with the Bridegroom and the need for purity. The church as "family" (Ephesians 2:19) illustrates *fellowship*, not just with each other but with the Godhead. The church as "temple"

But What Is the Church?

(Ephesians 2:20-22) points to its intrinsic holiness as *God's dwelling place*.

Is it all that important to accurately define just what the church is? Actually, the danger of failing to do so can hardly be overstated. If a true church exists, if our connection to that church is a matter of our personal salvation, and if those churches called "Babylon" are doomed to destruction, we had better get this church thing sorted out. On the other hand, if church is nothing more than a cozy fellowship of the likeminded, we need trouble ourselves no further.

In this chapter we will focus on how the Bible defines the church. It doesn't matter whether we call it the true church, the professed church, the remnant church, the lukewarm church, or the visible church; if it doesn't measure up to the Bible definition, we will have to conclude it is a counterfeit. For our purposes now, we will call it "God's church." We will look at ten characteristics rather briefly and study some in greater depth in the following chapters.

1. God's church is a divine institution designed and built by Jesus. Jesus is the great Church Builder. "On this rock I will build My church" (Matthew 16:18), He declares. He is not only the Architect, He is the Foundation (1 Corinthians 3:11), the Chief Cornerstone (Ephesians 2:20), the Senior Pastor (1 Peter 5:4), and the General Conference President (Ephesians 5:23).

Jesus created the church in Eden when He told Satan, "I will put enmity between you and the woman" (Genesis 3:15). "God had a church when Adam and Eve and Abel accepted and hailed with joy the good news that Jesus was their Redeemer" (*The Upward Look*, p. 228). Adam was its first priest; Eve, "the mother of all living," its enduring mystical symbol. Cain, their firstborn, would become the church's first apostate; Abel, its first martyr. How quickly the battle is joined!

Jesus chose Abraham as the human founder of the patriarchal church. "I will make you a great nation; I will bless you . . . and in you all the families of the earth shall be blessed" (Genesis 12:2, 3). Jesus founded the church in the wilderness with Moses as its leader. "For you are a holy people to the Lord your God, and the Lord has chosen you to be a people for Himself, a special treasure above all the peoples who are on the face of the earth" (Deuteronomy 14:2). Jesus created the Christian church when He selected and ordained His disciples (Luke 9:1). He said, "You did not choose Me, but I chose you" (John 15:16). During His ministry, several of His references to the "kingdom" can be understood as describing the church, the visible home for the kingdom of grace.

"God has a church. It is not the great cathedral [not that worldwide church known for its magnificent places of worship], neither is it the national establishment [not those powerful state churches that rule over the consciences of men], neither is it the various denominations [the multitude of Protestant denominations that have set the Bible aside in favor of tradition]; it is the people who love God and keep His commandments" (*The Upward Look*, p. 315). Further, she says, "Human might and human wisdom did not establish the church of God, and neither can they destroy it" ("A Sin-Pardoning Saviour," *The Pacific Union Recorder*, December 8, 1904).

So, based on past history, it is reasonable to conclude that somewhere in this world today Jesus has a church, either under construction or finished and occupied.

2. God's church is message, messengers, and mission. "And Jesus came and spoke to them, saying, . . . 'Go therefore and make disciples of all the nations, baptizing them in the name of the Father and of the Son and of the Holy Spirit, teaching them to observe all things that I have commanded you, and lo, I am with you always, even to the end of the age'" (Matthew 28:18-20). Jesus specifies the *message*: "all things I have commanded"; the *messengers*: "you" (every believer); and the *mission*: "go, make disciples of all nations, baptize and teach."

God has always had a special message to communicate to every generation. The church's mission is to give that message. It cannot justify its existence on any other grounds. Churches that are saying the same things ought to unite; those that have nothing of importance to say should consider going out of business. To discover the true church is to discover a church with a message that is crucial to one's salvation—a message that can be obtained nowhere else. That church will have a present revelation of Bible truth, sometimes referred to as "present truth," or "testing truth."

History shows that, however fiercely opposed by Satan, the message has gone out to those who were supposed to hear it. Noah preached the coming of the Flood and challenged his hearers to show their faith by boarding the ark. Amid the prevailing idolatry of his time, Abraham proclaimed the one unseen God. Through Moses, the church in the wilderness presented the plan of salvation through types and symbols. Paul's church preached the crucified, risen, resurrected, and returning Christ. Luther's church preached justification by faith. Wesley's preached sanctification.

God has not changed. Right now, somewhere in our world is "the church of the living God, the pillar and ground of the truth" (1 Timothy 3:15). "The church has been made the depository of precious truth" ("The Vine and the Branches," *Signs of the Times*, June 1, 1891). The word "depository" is most significant. It is the bank where one goes to find the coin of truth.

3. God's true church has an address. Any discussion of the church raises the issue of the visible and invisible church. Jesus recognized the existence of the "invisible church" when He said, "Other sheep I have which are not of this fold; them also I must bring, and they will hear My voice; and there will be one flock and one shepherd" (John 10:16). Paul may have been recognizing the existence of the invisible church when he speaks of the "whole family in heaven and earth" (Ephesians 3:15), or when he acknowledges that "since the creation of the world" there have been those who have understood something about God's "invisible attributes" through the things of nature (Romans 1:19-20).

The Church That Does Not Fall

An invisible church exists in the sense that there have always been people, churched and un-churched, who have walked in all the light they had and will be judged accordingly. Ty Gibson observes that "this [invisible] church is not an organized movement. You cannot hold membership in it. There are no earthly books that maintain a record of its names. It has no human leadership, no planned mission, and no system of discipline."[1]

But Jesus is not satisfied with that. His desire is to give to all the blessing of the fullest revelation of truth possible, to bring His "other sheep" into one fold, so that all become one flock under the care of one Shepherd. After all, the Good Shepherd risked His life to rescue the one lost sheep for the very reason that it was not in the fold!

That one fold has always been an identifiable entity in the world. The altars of Abraham, the wilderness tabernacle, the temple, the various synagogues, the churches planted by the apostles—all were material structures in geographical locations where God met with His people. Jesus went to worship in just such a location every Sabbath (Luke 4:16).

In the New Testament, the term church is used to describe believers assembled for worship in a specific place (1 Corinthians 11:18); believers living in a certain locality (1 Corinthians 16:1; Galatians 1:2; 1 Thessalonians 2:14); a group of believers assembling in the home of an individual (1 Corinthians 16:19; Colossians 4:15); a group of congregations existing in a given geographical area (Acts 9:31); and the whole body of believers scattered throughout the world (Matthew 16:18; 1 Corinthians 10:32). The "body" metaphor stands strongly against the idea of the invisible church being the "true" church. A body, by definition, exists only when all the body parts are brought together as a visible, living entity.

From a human perspective, God's choice of men or nations to be the nucleus of His church may seem wholly arbitrary and veiled in mystery. Why did He choose Abraham instead of Melchizedek or Job? Why did He choose

But What Is the Church?

Palestine instead of Italy or Greece? Why didn't Jesus choose Nicodemus, Paul, and Stephen to be part of the twelve? Why did He choose the United States over Canada or Brazil to cradle the Advent Movement? We cannot challenge those choices. They are the rightful exercise of the One who is the Head of the church.

The church on earth has always had an address and still does today. How could it possibly be otherwise? How can God say to those in spiritual Babylon, "Come out" (Revelation 18:4), unless He provides a place for them to come in to? The physical facilities do not have to be fancy, but they do need to exist, whether that's a stained-glass edifice or a thatched hut.

4. God's church is organized for service. The church exists for service, and it must organize its human and material resources to do that effectively. Suppose you were to take a severely injured person from the scene of an accident into the nearest town and stop to ask directions to the hospital. "We're sorry," you are told, "but we operate a *home* hospital. Our hospital is scattered throughout this city in various medical workers' homes. You get x-rayed on Maple Street, receive transfusions on Skyline Drive, and have surgery on Lincoln Avenue." It is just as preposterous to think that isolated individuals, or even home churches and independent ministries, are sufficient to carry out the monumental assignment of conducting a worldwide medical, educational, publishing, and evangelistic ministry.

Certainly, it cannot be said that Jesus is opposed to organization. He organized the twelve disciples and sent them out to cover assigned territory in a systematic way (Luke 9:1-6). Later He organized seventy disciples into thirty-five teams to visit territory where He planned to do follow up (Luke 10:1). He did not work in a haphazard fashion; He was the model administrator.

Following Pentecost, the church in Jerusalem grew rapidly, from 120 (Acts 1:15) to 3,000 (Acts 2:41) to 5,000 (Acts 4:4). "It is evident that these first Christian believers acted as a corporate and visible community. They 'devoted themselves to the apostles' teaching' (Acts 2:42), had fellowship with one another (verse 43), observed the ordinance of baptism (verses 38, 41) and the Lord's Supper (verse 42), met for prayer (verse 42), worshiped together (verse 46), and contributed to the support of the needy (verses 44, 45). These are undoubtedly characteristics of a visible and, however loosely organized, local church."[2]

It is most instructive to notice how God honored His organized church in its early history. When Paul arrived in Damascus following his highway encounter with Jesus, he was blind, humbled, and filled with remorse. Even though Jesus looked upon Paul as "a chosen vessel of Mine to bear My name before Gentiles, kings, and the children of Israel" (Acts 9:15), He did not personally instruct him in the principles of Christianity. That could easily have had the effect of fostering an independent nature already too natural for Paul and tempted him to start his own "Pauline Christian Church."

Instead, Jesus graciously directed him to the home of a disciple named Judas who lived on a "street called Straight" (Acts 9:11). That address, in turn, was given to another disciple named Ananias with instructions to go and minister to Paul. "Thus," Ellen White says, "Jesus gave sanction to the authority of His organized church, and placed Saul in connection with His appointed agencies on earth. Christ had now a church as His representative on earth, and to it belonged the work of directing the repentant sinner in the way of life" (*The Acts of the Apostles*, p. 122).

Notice that, even though the church was in its infancy and under severe persecution, it was still called God's "organized church." Even in its underground status, the believers recognized the need for order and lines of authority, and God honored that embryonic organization.

As the early church grew, the believers recognized the need for expanding the organizational structure, and so they selected and ordained elders, deacons, and deaconesses (Acts 6:4, 20:17, 28; Titus 1:5-7). "The organization of the church at Jerusalem was to serve as a model for the

But What Is the Church?

organization of churches in every other place where messengers of truth should win converts to the gospel" (*The Acts of the Apostles*, p. 91). Growing up as they had with the Old Testament scriptures, it was natural that system and order would be a part of the very fabric of their lives. The camp of the Israelites—laid out in exact order with its people organized by tens, fifties, hundreds, thousands, and tribes, as directed by Jesus Himself—could well have served as a conceptual model for the early Christians to follow.

In spite of such overwhelming evidence, there are still those today who view the organized church as an evil that ought to be dispensed with. If they can envision the church taking the gospel to the world without leadership and structure, they need to share their management plan. History teaches that message, mission, and organization cannot be separated without destroying all three.

5. God's church has authority. "The church is God's delegated authority upon earth. Christ has said: 'Whatsoever ye shall bind on earth shall be bound in heaven: and whatsoever ye shall loose on earth shall be loosed in heaven.' There is altogether too little respect paid to the opinion of members of the same church.... The church is a power which should control its individual members. ... Unless the advice and counsel of the church can be respected, it is indeed powerless" (*Testimonies for the Church*, vol. 5, p. 107). I'll address this topic further in chapter ten.

6. God's church is composed of members, both good and bad. No teaching of the Bible is clearer—those looking for a perfect, Bible-based message of truth are to be commended, but those looking for a perfect people have not read or believed the Bible. The parable of the dragnet (Matthew 13:47), the parable of the wheat and tares (Matthew 13:24-30), the parable of the sheep and goats (Matthew 25:31-46), and the parable of the ten virgins (Matthew 25:1-13), all teach the same lesson: the converted and unconverted will be in the church until separated by the great Judge according to heaven's timetable.

We must not allow ourselves to be overcome with discouragement, because both good and bad are gathered into the church. Let's not focus so much on the weeds and goats that we forget about the wheat and sheep. Bad members in the church do not necessarily make its message and mission bad. The presence of Judas did not derail the mission of Christ's first church. A dramatic change is coming. The church militant will become the church triumphant. There will be more about that in chapter four.

7. God's church is a caring fellowship. The Bible's picture of the early church is one of togetherness. In Acts 2:42, fellowship is placed on the same line with doctrine. "They continued steadfastly in the apostles' doctrine and fellowship." If doctrine alone made a church, we could all stay home and be kept orthodox by reading official statements of belief. But God knows how much we need the warm handclasp of another, the sharing of experience, the testing of our ideas, and the submitting of one to another. He knows these are necessary for faith to be nurtured and hope to be kept alive.

We would find it instructive and encouraging to bring together and carefully consider all the "one-another" texts in the New Testament. We find that we are to love one another, forgive one another, comfort one another, pray for one another, etc. God's servant Ellen White says, "We are all children of God, mutually dependent upon one another for happiness" ("Christian Work," *Review and Herald*, October 10, 1882).

Secular organizations care about their members' social and physical needs. They might even provide scholarships for their members' children, pay for vacations, furnish health and fitness programs, and offer in-service training for occupational advancement. But only the church cares about where the individual will spend eternity. Only the church is interested in preparing each person to face the judgment. That is caring at the deepest level.

8. God's church is a place to worship and to learn how to worship. Jesus says, "Where two or three are gathered

But What Is the Church?

together in My name, I am there in the midst of them" (Matthew 18:20). The church is where Jesus is. "The presence of the High and Holy One who inhabiteth eternity can alone constitute a church" (*The Upward Look*, p. 315). More light and power can come to that microscopic fellowship than to all the independent Christians in the world who are trying to survive apart from the church.

The church not only provides us with a place to worship, its duty is to teach us how to worship the true God in spirit and in truth. Jesus says "the Father is seeking such to worship Him" (John 4:23). If our understanding of Bible prophecy is correct, the issue in the last days *is* worship. As the scroll unrolls, I believe we are going to learn that the *way* we worship will be as crucial as the *day* on which we worship. That's the subject of chapter fourteen.

9. God's church is a place of multiplied power. "And when they had prayed, the place where they had assembled together was shaken; and they were filled with the Holy Spirit, and they spoke the word of God with boldness" (Acts 4:31). We may not fully understand how or why; nevertheless, it is one of the ground rules in the great controversy that multiplying the prayer multiplies the power.

God never intended that one person should face the armies of hell alone. In the church, we are to seek out others whose praise and prayers and tears can mingle with our own as we wrestle for victory. It is the devil's strategy to keep believers separated from each other and downplay the importance of church membership and fellowship. He seeks to isolate us and prey on our aloneness. We need to remove the walls that separate us and experience the multiplied power of fellowship in Christ.

Robert Luccock, in his book *If God Be For Us*, speaks to the power of fellowship in the church. "We kneel where others have knelt and then rise to go out victors over the destructive power of alcohol, sex, temper, hate, weakness, and fear because they found at the heart of the Church One in whose grip they could handle these things. The

Church is the company of faithful where this power lives. It is a great thing to walk where they walked, kneel where they bowed. You may feel this power somewhere outside the Church. But it always comes as the overflow *from* the church, a legacy received *through* the Church, and unless it leads back *into* the Church and joins the body whence it came, it shrivels and dies."[3]

Also, multiplying the *gifts* multiplies the power. No person has every spiritual gift, but the church does (Romans 12; 1 Corinthians 12; Ephesians 4). Every spiritual gift is necessary in carrying forward the mission of the church. The gifts of our fellow believers are also necessary to our own spiritual advancement. "The church is a Christian society formed for the members composing it, that each member may enjoy the assistance of all the graces and talents of the other members . . . The church is united in the holy bonds of fellowship in order that each member may be benefited by the influence of the other" (*Selected Messages*, bk. 3, pp. 15, 16).

The multiplying of power through prayer and the combining of gifts plays out in very practical ways that can be illustrated best by imagining what life would be like if we were not connected to the organized church.

The elders of what church would I call if I or a family member were to become seriously ill (James 5:17)?

If I were to have unresolved difficulties with others, how would I comply with Jesus' direction to "tell it to the church" (Matthew 18:17)?

When my children or my neighbors are ready for baptism, to whom would I look to perform that rite, and with what church would they unite (Acts 2:47)?

How do I decide whether or not my interpretations of the Bible are correct (Acts 15:6-21)?

Where is the storehouse to which I would bring my tithes and offerings, and who are the ministers that it would support (Malachi 3:10)?

Who or what agency would build schools for my children, hospitals for my sick and injured, and take the gospel to the entire world on my behalf (Matthew 28:18-20)?

But What Is the Church?

And perhaps most important of all, who would hold me accountable for faithfulness to my baptismal vows (Romans 15:14; Colossians 3:16; 2 Timothy 4:2)?

10. **God's church is an agency for the believer's salvation.** "The Lord added to the church daily those who were being saved" (Acts 2:47). Salvation and church membership are closely related, but we will hold our discussion of that crucial issue for chapter eleven.

At this point I suppose one could argue that several religious organizations in our world might meet the majority of the foregoing qualifications for "church." Many churches feel strongly about taking their version of the gospel to the world, sincerely believe they are in compliance with the Bible, are well organized and visible, and constitute a caring, nurturing fellowship. Does that mean they can count themselves as approved of God and offering a safe haven for the lost? If so, how do they relate to what the Bible calls "the remnant"? That's next.

Discussion Questions:

1. Do you feel the church to which you belong is securely founded on Christ and His Word?
2. How would you identify the church's message and mission today? Do you often think of yourself as a messenger?
3. How important are physical facilities to a church family and to the community to which it witnesses?
4. In your experience, has the church's exercise of authority been generally too weak? Too domineering? About right?
5. Would it be better for God to maintain a sharp separation between the obedient and disobedient in the church today? How large would the church be if He did?
6. Do you honestly believe the majority of the members in your church care about you—care about both your physical and spiritual well-being?
7. Have you witnessed the tremendous power there is in combining your spiritual gifts with those of other

members in your church? If not, what can you do to bring that power into play?

Endnotes

1 Ty Gibson, *Abandon Ship?* (Boise: Pacific Press Publishing Association, 1997), 50.
2 *Handbook of Seventh-day Adventist Theology* (Hagerstown: Review and Herald Publishing Association, 2000), 546.
3 Robert E. Luccock, *If God Be For Us* (New York: Harper and Brothers, 1954), 152- 153.

Chapter Three

AND WHO ARE THE REMNANT?

"Unless the Lord of hosts had left to us a very small remnant, we would have become like Sodom, we would have been made like Gomorrah" (Isaiah 1:9).

A remnant is a fragment, a small part of the original, often considered of little value. It is a piece of cloth at the end of the bolt that is usually thrown into the bargain bin. The remnant designation is used by Isaiah, Jeremiah, Ezekiel, Joel, Amos, and John the Revelator to describe those faithful few who maintain their loyalty to God in the midst of near-universal apostasy.

But if you were to ask most non-Adventist Christians if they believe their church is "the remnant," the answer would likely be no; some because they find the designation elitist and offensive; others because they have no idea what you're talking about.

Those same responses are also being heard from some Seventh-day Adventists, especially the younger members of the church. They may see the remnant idea as a bit of ego left over from the enthusiasm of the pioneers. Besides, they have been schooled in social sensitivity and political correctness and are loath to ascribe to themselves a title of honor and distinction while leaving others to flounder in something called "Babylon."

Seventh-day Adventists have, throughout their history, considered themselves to be the fulfillment of the prophesied remnant in Revelation 12:17, KJV: "And the dragon was wroth with the woman, and went to make war with the remnant of her seed, which keep the commandments of God, and have the testimony of Jesus Christ." In fact, in the 1860s Adventists gave consideration to calling themselves "The Remnant." Some might find it surprising, therefore, to learn that it was not until the General Conference session in 1980 that a statement dealing with the concept of the remnant was included in the church's fundamental beliefs. It is one of our newer doctrinal statements.

Here it is, fundamental belief number thirteen: "The universal church is composed of all who truly believe in Christ, but in the last days, a time of widespread apostasy, a remnant has been called out to keep the commandments of God and the faith of Jesus. This remnant announces the arrival of the judgment hour, proclaims salvation through Christ, and heralds the approach of His second advent. This proclamation is symbolized by the three angels of Revelation 14; it coincides with the work of judgment in heaven and results in a work of repentance and reform on earth. Every believer is called to have a personal part in this worldwide witness."[1]

God has always had a remnant—sometimes just barely! Only eight survived the Flood; only three escaped the destruction of Sodom; only two adults out of the million or more who exited Egypt eventually set foot in the Promised Land. During the apostasy of Israel under Ahab and Jezebel, those who remained faithful shrank to somewhere around seven thousand. During the Babylonian captivity, Daniel and his friends were among a tiny minority who stood for their faith at the risk of their lives.

Interestingly, even during the period of the Thyatira church, the church of the "Dark Ages," Jesus commended a faithful remnant. "Now to you I say, and to the rest [or *remnant*; same word as in Revelation 12:17] in Thyatira, as many as do not have this doctrine [of Jezebel], who have not known the depths of Satan . . ." (Revelation 2:24). The remnant here is undoubtedly a reference to groups like the Waldenses, Albigenses, Hugenots, Hussites, and others who remained faithful to God under great hardship and severe persecution.

But when we talk about the end-time remnant church, what do we mean? We mean that God has not changed, and that somewhere in this world we can find the lamp of

And Who Are the Remnant?

truth still burning, that somewhere a group exists whose biblical teachings stand in sharp contrast to the general apostasy. If they are faithful to their calling, such a group, though small, should not be that hard to find. It should be as simple as finding the healthiest, happiest, holiest people in the world, right? But maybe we need something a bit more objective.

As we turn to the Bible for a more precise definition, remember that the criteria we reviewed in the last chapter that identify the church in general also apply to the remnant—it is founded by Jesus; it is visible; it is a mixture of the converted and the unconverted; it is organized for service, etc. Following are seven identifying marks of the remnant.

1. The end-time remnant arises right on time in fulfillment of Bible prophecy. The twelfth chapter of Revelation outlines the great controversy between Christ and Satan. It tells of war in heaven and the casting to earth of the arch-rebel and his cohorts (verses 7-9). It tells of the fierce battle for the souls of human beings (verses 10-12), of the hatred of Satan against the Christ child (verses 1-5), of the relentless persecution of the followers of Christ for 1,260 years (verses 6; 13-16), and of Satan's hatred of the faithful believers who live in the end time (verse 17).

According to this prophecy, the remnant makes its appearance after the end of the 1,260 years of the great tribulation, which ended in 1798 (Revelation 12:6, 14). They must come into being by the end of the 2300-day prophecy, which ended in 1844, if they are to give the judgment-hour message of Revelation 14:6-8. That message and the two that accompany it are the most solemn warnings ever given to mortals. When God has a message to give, He raises up messengers. The prophesied remnant appeared on time.

2. The remnant keeps all the commandments of God. Revelation 14:12 places the remnant in sharp contrast to those who serve Satan and worship the beast. The remnant, through faith in Jesus, keeps the commandments of God (John 15:10) while the rest of the world rebels against His righteous laws and receives the mark of the beast (Revelation 13:16).

Millions of Christians profess to believe in the Ten Commandments, but it is only a profession. They pick and choose, they rewrite, they add and subtract. They give lip service to the letter but deny the spirit. Only the remnant, through the strength which Christ imparts, obeys from the heart all of God's commandments, including the fourth. They walk as Jesus walked (1 John 2:6). They follow the Lamb wherever He goes (Revelation 14:4). Jesus kept the seventh-day Sabbath (Luke 4:16); they keep the seventh-day Sabbath (Revelation 12:17).

Isaiah looked down the corridor of time and foretold the coming of those who would "raise up the foundation of many generations" and be called "the Repairer of the Breach, the Restorer of Streets to Dwell In" (Isaiah 58:12). The very next verse speaks of Sabbath reform. Those searching for the remnant must find a church who is putting the fourth commandment back in its rightful place among the other ten.

3. The remnant has the faith of Jesus. Jesus had absolute confidence in the trustworthiness of the Bible. "The scripture cannot be broken," He said in John 10:35. "Do not think that I came to destroy the Law or the Prophets . . ." (Matthew 5:17). And that's the kind of faith the remnant have. They have faith sufficient to believe every truth of the Bible—the very same truths Jesus believed and taught.

Jesus had an obedient faith. "My food is to do the will of Him who sent Me," He declared (John 4:34). "Not as I will, but as You will," He prayed in Gethsemane (Matthew 26:39). Just so, the faith of those who constitute the remnant will be more than mere profession; it will be a faith that works, a faith that leads to active, loving obedience.

The NIV translation of Revelation 14:12 needs to be considered here: "This calls for patient endurance on the part of the saints who obey God's commandments and remain faithful to Jesus." Whether one reads the text as describing those who "have faith like Jesus," "have faith in Jesus," or "remain faithful to Jesus," the end product is the same: Here is a group whose model in all things pertaining to spiritual life is Jesus.

4. The remnant has the gift of prophecy. "And the dragon was enraged with the woman, and he went to make war with the rest of her offspring, who . . . have the testimony of Jesus Christ" (Revelation 12:17). "For the testimony of Jesus is the spirit of prophecy" (Revelation 19:10). The true remnant will have every spiritual gift, including the gift of prophecy. The prophet or prophets associated with that movement will be in strict compliance with the Bible tests of a true prophet (Deuteronomy 18:22; Isaiah 8:20; Matthew 7:20; 1 John 4:1-3).

One's search for the remnant is not finished if it comes up short here. We *must* find a church with the prophetic gift. There must be in its ranks, or in its end-time history, one who was inspired of God to lead, to teach, and to foretell the future.

5. The remnant proclaims the three angels' messages. Arising in the period following the close of the great tribulation (1798), the remnant would be identified by their proclamation of the true gospel, the investigative judgment, Christ's high-priestly ministry in heaven's sanctuary, the fall of Babylon, and the warning against receiving the mark of the beast (Revelation 14:6-12).

Even though we speak of the remnant *church*, the phenomenon we are trying to describe may be more properly designated as a "movement." The dictionary definition of a church is "a body of believers;" a movement is defined as "an organized effort to promote or attain an end or goal." Whereas "church" is often associated with an organization that is established, formal, and satisfied (or even lethargic); "movement" suggests vitality, intense activity, and deep commitment. The urgency of the remnant's assignment to take the three angels' messages to the entire world "in this generation" makes the movement label most fitting.

6. The end-time remnant is the special target of the wrath of Satan. "The dragon was angry with the woman." The true remnant may or may not be seen as experiencing persecution, depending on the time and place of one's search. But at any given moment since the beginning of their history, the remnant have been treated with contempt and abuse in some part of our world and will be so treated throughout the world before Christ returns. "Yes, and all who desire to live godly in Christ Jesus will suffer persecution" (2 Timothy 3:12).

7. The remnant is the special object of God's love and care. God's providential care for His people will be a witness to an unbelieving world. "The remnant of Israel shall . . . feed their flocks and lie down, and no one shall make them afraid" (Ephesians 3:13). The mission of the end-time remnant will advance with such rapidity that the world in general will recognize them as having the favor of God. "God also bearing witness both with signs and wonders, with various miracles, and gifts of the Holy Spirit . . ." (Hebrews 2:4).

Who is it?

So, we ask: Does a church exist in our world today that meets these seven Bible characteristics that identify God's true remnant?

What church arose at the very time that the antitypical Day of Atonement began in 1844 in fulfillment of Daniel 8:14? The Methodists were a hundred years too early, the Jehovah's Witnesses forty years too late. The Mormons were pretty much on time but had no understanding of Jesus' high-priestly ministry and did nothing to restore the Sabbath.

What church keeps all the commandments of God, including the fourth, which specifies the seventh day of the week as the true Sabbath according to Exodus 20:8-11? The Jews do, but they do not have faith in Jesus. The Seventh-day Baptists do, but they do not have the Spirit of Prophecy.

What church has the faith of Jesus, a faith that surrenders completely to the will of God as Jesus did in Gethsemane, and renders active, loving obedience to all

And Who Are the Remnant?

that God asks? Many churches might make this claim, but they either do not accept the entire Bible or are selective in what they choose to obey.

What church has the gift of prophecy—not a part-time, hit-or-miss gift but a prophet whose teachings align perfectly with those of Scripture? Some groups have made this claim, but when challenged by the Bible tests of a true prophet, they fail miserably.

What church is proclaiming at this very hour in virtually every country on this planet the three angels' messages of Revelation 14? Most churches have no understanding of these messages and therefore no interest in proclaiming them.

What church, according to the prophecies of Daniel and Revelation, will feel the special wrath of Satan? The Jews, particularly, have suffered terribly. Nearly every church, at some time in its history, has been persecuted by antagonistic civil or religious powers. But to qualify as the remnant, a church must suffer persecution for the reason the Bible specifies. The remnant is a New Testament Christian church that is persecuted for keeping *all* the commandments of God (Revelation 12:14).

What church is the special object of God's favor as evidenced by the fact that, though small in numbers, it has a medical, educational, evangelistic, and publishing work second to none among all the churches of the world?

To all of these questions we can answer without hesitation: the Seventh-day Adventist church. Of the seven foregoing identifying marks, what other church in all the world can rightly claim that even one or two, much less six or seven, accurately defines them?

Perhaps the most unqualified endorsement of all we have been saying is this: "Seventh-day Adventists have been chosen by God as a peculiar people, separate from the world. By the great cleaver of truth He has cut them out from the quarry of the world and brought them into connection with Himself. He has made them His representatives and has called them to be ambassadors for Him in the last work of salvation. The greatest wealth of truth ever entrusted to mortals, the most solemn and fearful warnings ever sent by God to man, have been committed to them to be given to the world" (*Testimonies for the Church*, vol. 7, p. 138).

We must hasten to add that each Seventh-day Adventist must qualify personally with respect to remnant identity. The foregoing qualifications can be used in a somewhat theoretical way to identify the remnant church; however, the crucial question is: Do they describe you and me?

Ultimately, the remnant is not what we claim, but who we are. If the foregoing criteria do indeed define the remnant, then we do not have the privilege of picking and choosing. For instance, we cannot claim remnant identity while rejecting the prophetic gift or by failing to follow the Lamb wherever He goes, including His present ministry in heaven's sanctuary. "We profess to have more truth than other denominations; yet if this does not lead to greater consecration, to purer, holier lives, of what benefit is it to us? It would be better for us never to have seen the light of truth than to profess to accept it and not be sanctified through it" (*Testimonies for the Church*, vol. 5, p. 620).

Neither smugness nor a false humility

We must continually guard against smugness and self-righteousness on the one hand and a false humility on the other. It is part of our carnal nature to desire recognition. It is not inconceivable that someone would join God's true church so they could lay claim to some kind of spiritual aristocracy to lord over others. True Christians find that wholly repugnant. We are all sinners saved by grace.

But the other extreme is just as bad. And that is to deny our high calling and great privileges. "You are a chosen generation, a royal priesthood, a holy nation, His own special people, that you may proclaim the praises of Him who called you out of darkness into His marvelous light; who once were not a people but are now the people

And Who Are the Remnant?

of God, who had not obtained mercy but now have obtained mercy" (1 Peter 2:9, 10).

In light of that, how could anyone find the remnant identity so offensive that they would take the Seventh-day Adventist sign down from their church and hide behind some generic label? There were people of that mindset even in Ellen White's time. She writes, "A company was presented before me under the name of Seventh-day Adventists, who were advising that the banner or sign which makes us a distinctive people should not be held out so strikingly; for they claimed it was not the best policy in securing success to our institutions. This distinctive banner is to be borne through the world to the close of probation" (*Selected Messages*, bk. 2, p. 385).

There is, after all, no use in trying to hide. Regardless of their small size, the remnant will eventually be well known. "Our people have been regarded as too insignificant to be worthy of notice, but a change will come. The Christian world is now making movements which will necessarily bring commandment-keeping people into prominence" (*Testimonies for the Church*, vol. 5, p. 546).

There is certainly nothing intrinsically elitist or exclusive about the Seventh-day Adventist message. It is being taken to all races, rich and poor, learned and ignorant. All are invited; all are welcome. In the process of giving that message, we do not condemn those who have not yet heard. Seventh-day Adventists have never taught that only members of their denomination will be saved. They readily acknowledge that God has precious jewels in all churches and outside of any church. The problem lies in not keeping the question in proper chronological context. The question has a different answer today than it will have in some tomorrow.

As Gerhard Hasel has so well expressed it, "They too [those who walk in all the light they have] are the children of God. But until they join the commandment-keeping, faith-of-Jesus holding remnant, they are *not* part of the final remnant. *In the course of time* all children of God, whether in Christian churches or non-Christian religions, who listen to the Spirit of God and follow His wooings will be drawn by the faithful, global proclamation of the 'everlasting gospel' into the visible community of the final remnant of faith, which even now proclaims this message with power and conviction."[2]

Remnant identity will become increasingly clear in the closing up of the great controversy because of the Sabbath-Sunday issue. And in that issue, the just claims of God's law will be defended by Seventh-day Adventists alone. The time will come when all others will capitulate. The Jews, the Muslims, the Hindus—every person on the planet of whatever religious persuasion—will have yielded. Even avowed secularists and atheists will cave in to the overwhelming pressure.

"Those who honor the Bible Sabbath will be denounced as enemies of law and order, as breaking down the moral restraints of society, causing anarchy and corruption, and calling down the judgments of God upon the earth" (*The Great Controversy*, p. 592). Whatever happens to buildings and institutions, the true followers of Christ will be targeted because they are identified with the Bible Sabbath, the most distinguishing mark of the organized Seventh-day Adventist church.

In the third century, St. Cyprian wrote the following to a friend: "This seems a cheerful world, Donatus, when I view it from this fair garden, under the shadow of these vines. But if I climbed some great mountain and looked out over the wide lands, you know very well what I would see. Brigands on the high roads, pirates on the seas, in the amphitheaters men murdered to please the applauding crowds, under all roofs misery and selfishness. It really is a bad world, Donatus, an incredibly bad world. Yet in the midst of it I have found a quiet and holy people. They have discovered a joy which is a thousand times better than any pleasure of this sinful life. They are despised and persecuted, but they care not. They have overcome the world. These people, Donatus, are the Christians—and I am one of them."[3]

And Who Are the Remnant?

Sounds like someone who had found the remnant. And that can be the experience of all, who, in their search for truth and wholeness, find a place of peace and rest in the fold of the end-time remnant under the care of the Great Shepherd.

God, who saw our day with perfect clarity, gave His prophets two designations for the end-time church: remnant and Laodicea. Do those words really define the same group, or does one cancel out the other?

Discussion Questions:

1. The fundamental belief statement that defines the Seventh-day Adventist doctrine of the remnant does not specifically say that we believe it is the Seventh-day Adventist church. Should it?
2. Why do you think some Seventh-day Adventists seem to dislike the concept of the remnant?
3. When someone says, "remnant," the hearer tends to "think small." Can that be a hindrance to church growth? Is there reason not to believe the end-time remnant could number in the millions, even hundreds of millions?
4. Do you think it is likely that the remnant will have the gift of prophecy manifest in its midst again before Jesus comes? Are there Bible texts to support that?

Endnotes

1 *Seventh-day Adventists Believe* . . . (Hagerstown: Review and Herald Publishing Association, 1988), 152.

2 Gerhard Hasel, "Who Are the Remnant?" *Adventists Affirm* (Fall 1993): 31. (emphasis supplied)

3 Howard Luccock, *If God Be for Us* (New York: Harper and Brothers, 1954), 161.

Chapter Four

LAODICEA IS NOT A BAD WORD

"As many as I love, I rebuke and chasten. Therefore be zealous and repent" (Revelation 3:19).

Following a sermon in which Laodicea and Laodiceans received a sound thrashing, a friend of mine said to the speaker, "I'm sure glad I'm a Laodicean!"

The speaker was aghast. "Why would you say that?" he asked.

"Because," my friend replied, "if I were not a Laodicean, I would not be a part of God's true church at all!"

Was he right?

In Seventh-day Adventist circles, the words "Laodicea" and "Laodicean" carry some pretty negative connotations. And it is true; the Bible does not paint a rosy picture. "Because you are lukewarm, and neither cold nor hot, I will vomit you out of My mouth. . . . [You] do not know that you are wretched, miserable, poor, blind, and naked" (Revelation 3:16, 17). Jesus uses six uncomplimentary adjectives to describe Laodicea's spiritual condition, and Adventists have evidently decided that "lukewarm" is the least threatening. (Can you imagine belonging to the *miserable* church?)

Nevertheless, taken as a whole, here is a graphic description of the most unkempt, ragged, sightless, and homeless refugee imaginable. And when the spiritual implications are understood, it's hard to blame anyone for wanting to distance themselves from anyone or anything that is associated with Laodicea.

From the time Ellen and James White first applied the Laodicean message to Seventh-day Adventists in 1856,[1] the response of members has been to make personal application of its counsel, deny that it has any particular

Laodicea Is Not a Bad Word

application to the church today, or pull away from such a spiritually destitute group and attempt to find or form one with more positive traits. Let's see which of these positions is warranted by the facts.

Fact No. 1: Laodicea represents a period of time in the history of the church.

Adventists have always believed that the seven churches of Revelation 2 and 3 represent the Christian church through various periods of its history. "The names of the seven churches," Ellen White writes, "are symbolic of the church in different periods of the Christian Era. The number 7 indicates completeness, and is symbolic of the fact that the messages extend to the end of time, while the symbols used reveal the condition of the church at different periods in the history of the world" (*The Acts of the Apostles*, p. 585).

Here is a typical chronological outline:[2]

- Ephesus, 31-100, the apostolic church (Revelation 2:1-7)

- Smyrna, 100-313, the persecuted church (Revelation 2:8-11)

- Pergamos, 313-538, the compromising church (Revelation 2:12-17)

- Thyatira, 538-1565, the apostate (or persecuting) church (Revelation 2:18-29)

- Sardis, 1565-1740, the reformation church (Revelation 3:1-6)

- Philadelphia, 1740-1844, the loving church (Revelation 3:7-13)

- Laodicea, 1844 to the Second Coming, the judgment-hour church (Revelation 3:14-22)

When trying to understand Laodicea, we must first understand that the word designates *a period of time in the Christian era*. It is not in itself a pejorative term. Laodicea is the last of seven. No church will follow Laodicea.

The Church That Does Not Fall

We can put this matter to rest once and forever. There is no eighth church. The remnant either did or did not arise in the immediate post-1844 era. If it did, one cannot start something today and call it "historic Adventism" or "the true remnant" or "the remnant of the remnant" and make it fit the prophetic picture. That will not work. If there is an eighth church, it is the one that gathers on the sea of glass. We should feel a sense of great joy and anticipation just to know we are living in the days of the last church—the one that will greet a returning Savior.

Why did Jesus choose the church in the city of Laodicea to represent the last church? He did so because the term itself means "the judging of the people." That should make our mouths drop open. The name itself is a prophecy given two thousand years ago, describing the church that would proclaim the judgment-hour message of Revelation 14:6 and 7! The time period assigned to Laodicea is beyond question.

Fact No. 2: Laodicea represents a spiritual condition of the church in that time period.

Jesus found things to commend and things to correct in most of the seven churches. Every church except Laodicea receives a commendation. All receive counsel and encouragement, most receive rebukes or warnings, and without exception, all receive the promise of a reward.

The actual city of Laodicea in apostolic times was a center of trade, manufacturing, banking, and considerable wealth. A leading health resort, Laodicea offered mineral water and warm baths. It had a medical college and produced an eye medicine called collyrium. Laodicean sheep growers produced glossy black wool that was used to make robes that were worn with pride by Laodiceans.

Jesus' choice of Laodicea to represent the church today was no accident. Laodiceans were well-to-do, but Jesus calls them poor. Adventists are prone to take pride, not only in their nice schools, churches, and hospitals, but also in the great treasure of truth they possess. Jesus says we need the gold of faith and love. We do not lack

Laodicea Is Not a Bad Word

truth; rather, we need a loving relationship with Jesus that produces good works and the fruits of the Spirit.

The original Laodiceans were proud of their rich black robes, but Jesus says they are naked. Adventists can find themselves clothed in the black garments of pride and self-righteousness and overlook their need for the white robe of Christ's righteousness. Laodiceans produced a salve to treat eye disease; yet Jesus says they were still blind. With all their understanding of Bible truth, last-day Laodiceans can still be blind to their own spiritual condition. Only the eye salve of the Holy Spirit will make that clear to them.

Notice how Ellen White applies the Laodicean message to Seventh-day Adventists: "The message to the church of the Laodiceans applies especially to the people of God today. It is a message to professing Christians who have become so much like the world that no difference can be seen" (*SDA Bible Commentary*, vol. 7, p. 966). "The message to the Laodiceans is applicable to Seventh-day Adventists who have had great light and have not walked in the light" (*Selected Messages*, bk. 2, p. 66).

I trust the reader is noting that these statements are not all-inclusive. They are "if-the-shoe-fits-wear-it" statements. They are addressed to the worldly, the selfish, the egotistic. It seems obvious that God's messenger intended "Laodicean" and "lukewarm" to describe *individual* backslidden Seventh-day Adventists, and never meant those terms to describe a corrupt and rejected denomination.

We might have asked the apostle Paul, "Aren't you ashamed to belong to a church (Ephesus) that has lost its first love?"

And Paul would no doubt have answered, "Well, I haven't lost mine!"

And so, throughout the history of the church there have been the faithful and unfaithful. Laodicea is no different, and leaving the church for a "pure" group will not change that.

Fact No. 3: Laodicea represents a message designed to correct their spiritual condition.

The Church That Does Not Fall

In these last days, the three angels' messages of Revelation 14:6-12 are God's message to the world; Revelation 3:14-21 is God's message to the remnant church. The message to Laodicea not only diagnoses the disease, it prescribes a cure. "I counsel you to buy from Me gold refined in the fire, that you may be rich; and white garments, that you may be clothed, that the shame of your nakedness may not be revealed; and anoint your eyes with eye salve, that you may see" (Revelation 3:18). The cure is gold for your poverty, white raiment for your nakedness, and eye salve for your blindness.

We cannot, at this time, explore this counsel in depth. However, I think it is important that we note at least three things about the message to Laodicea.

First, it is a message designed to correct and arouse to action. "As many as I love, I rebuke and chasten" (Revelation 3:19). We may wish it were not so, but the proof of love is correction. "This message must be borne to a lukewarm church by God's servants. It must arouse His people from their security and dangerous deception in regard to their real standing before God. This testimony, if received, will arouse to action and lead to self-abasement and confession of sins" (*Testimonies for the Church*, vol. 3, p. 259).

No church in the history of Christianity has been so rebuked and chastened as Laodicea! Not only do we have the Bible's correctives, but we have the immense volume of Spirit of Prophecy counsel to make us squirm—coming down, as it does, to "the minutiae of life" (*Testimonies for the Church*, vol. 5, p. 667). That chastening will be cheerfully submitted to by those who hang on for dear life to the first five words of Revelation 3:19: "As many as I love."

Second, it is a message that expresses hope. Clearly, neither Jesus nor the Holy Spirit, speaking through Ellen White, treats the Laodiceans as if they were beyond hope. "The counsel of the true Witness does not represent those who are lukewarm as in a hopeless case. There is yet a chance to remedy their state, and the Laodicean message is full of encouragement . . . There is hope for our churches if they will heed the message given to the Laodiceans" (*SDA Bible Commentary*, vol. 7, p. 966). God's purpose is the restoration of Laodicea, not its rejection. We need to join Him in that loving ministry.

Third, it is a message that speaks directly to each individual, calling for a personal decision. "Oh, how precious was this promise, as it was shown to me in vision! 'Behold, I stand at the door, and knock: if any man hear My voice, and open the door, I will come in to Him, and will sup with him, and he with Me.' Oh, the love, the wondrous love of God! After all our lukewarmness and sins He says: 'Return unto Me, and I will return unto thee, and will heal all thy backslidings.'. . . Some, I saw, would gladly return. Others will not let this message to the Laodicean church have its weight upon them" (*Testimonies for the Church*, vol. 1, pp. 143-144).

Notice, there are two groups: "some" and "others." Two classes are presented: Those whose self-righteousness and worldliness become incurable; and those who, although they were at one time deceived as to their true condition, wake up, repent, and welcome Jesus as a permanent resident in their innermost lives.

The threat of being "spued out" does not apply to the whole church. "'So then because thou art lukewarm, and neither cold nor hot, I will spue thee out of my mouth' (Revelation 3:16). What does this mean? That He will no longer present the name of such a one to His Father" (*The Upward Look*, p. 213).

God does not approve of anyone using the Laodicean message to discredit the church, to discourage the church, or to call members to separate from the church. "God has not given them any such burden of labor. They would tear down that which God would restore by the Laodicean message. He wounds only that He may heal, not cause to perish. The Lord lays upon no man a message that will discourage or dishearten the church. He reproves, He rebukes, He chastens, but it is only that He may restore and approve at last" (*Testimonies to Ministers and Gospel Workers*, pp. 22-23). "The Lord is merciful. He does not chastise His people because He hates them, but because He hates the sins they are committing" (*The Upward Look*, p. 240).

Fact No. 4: Laodicea is not Babylon.

While the message to Laodicea is full of hope, the message to Babylon is simply an announcement of its doom (Revelation 18). Although individual Laodiceans may continue in a backslidden state until the close of probation and, in heart, belong to Babylon or choose to leave and overtly join with Babylon, it cannot be said that they—Laodicea and Babylon—are one and the same.

Some see Laodicea as a church in apostasy, and therefore, they find it hard to understand how a church that makes Jesus want to vomit can be any different from fallen Babylon. We're going to deal with both Babylon and the apostasy question in the following chapters. Right now, I suggest that God's people today face two challenges: the first is to come out of Babylon; the second is to learn to love and work for Laodicea *within Laodicea*. We are called to work patiently and tirelessly to elevate the spiritual level of the church where we hold membership.

Listen to this: "Jesus is coming in, to give the individual members of the church the richest blessings, if they will open the door to Him. He does not once call them Babylon, nor ask them to come out, but He says, 'As many as I love, I rebuke and chasten'" (*Manuscript Releases*, vol. 1, p. 301). The solution is not to come out, but to open the door and let Jesus come in!

We live in a time never faced by any generation in exactly the same way since the great Flood. We face the close of probation. We face the final sifting and shaking of the church. And when we get to that point in time, there will be but two groups—the hot and the cold. The lukewarm will have become excited and involved in winning others, or they will have grown cold and drifted into Babylon. As the final chapter in earth's history is written, the church of God will be composed of those who hear and

Laodicea Is Not a Bad Word

heed the message to Laodicea and, under the power of the latter rain, warn the world of the coming judgment.

John the Revelator says, "The seven lampstands which you saw are the seven churches" (Revelation 1:20). Without question, *Laodicea* is one of those lampstands and is shining out into the moral darkness of these latter days. *Laodicea* has to be that church which, "enfeebled and defective, needing to be reproved, warned, and counseled, is the only object upon earth upon which Christ bestows His supreme regard." Surely, *Laodicea* is that last-day church which "is the depositary of the wealth of the riches of the grace of Christ, and through [whom] eventually will be made the final and full display of the love of God to the world that is to be lightened with its glory." Its place in history makes *Laodicea* that "one church in the world who is at the present time standing in the breach, and making up the hedge, building up the old waste places." (All quoted material in this paragraph was taken from *Testimonies to Ministers and Gospel Workers*, pp. 49-50.)

I invite you to do some serious pretending. Let's suppose you have been invited to attend Jesus' "New Disciples Church," and so on a sunny Sabbath morning, you make your way to the place of meeting. The service is in progress as you take your seat in the back of the room, where you can observe unnoticed the rest of the congregation. The Master is teaching an important truth, and you sit in rapt attention as do the others. Instinctively, you know you are where you ought to be.

But as you observe the other worshippers, you say to yourself, "I *know* these people! Bless his heart; there is Nathaniel, a guileless Israelite indeed! I see Mary, the mother of Jesus, with Lazarus and Martha seated beside her. Ah, yes, there's impulsive, hypocritical Peter. He talks a good line but is as unstable as a reed in the wind. There is Judas, a treacherous thief and betrayer. How did *he* get to be treasurer? Across the aisle sits Thomas with not even a mustard seed of faith. And right on the front row, as might be expected, are James and John, ambition personified, and with the shortest fuses in town."

The friend who invited you claims this is God's true church, but you wonder. Is this really the place God would have me worship? Is this the best place there is for spiritual nurturing and fellowship? Does God really expect me to return my tithe to *this* church?

Suddenly your reveries are interrupted, and your attention is riveted once again on the Speaker. "Where two or three are gathered together in My name," He is saying, "I am there in the midst of them" (Matthew 18:20). Ah, you say to yourself, I can put up with these fellow church members of mine just to meet with Jesus—to be where Jesus is in the middle of things! The church may not be perfect but we have a perfect Leader!

To those in Laodicea, Jesus says, "As many as I love . . ." Jesus loves everyone in Laodicea, those who hear and open the door, and those who keep the door shut tight. Do you and I love what He loves? Can we say with God's servant, "My interest is in this work; my life is interwoven with it. When Zion prospers, I am happy; if she languishes, I am sad"? (*Testimonies for the Church*, vol. 1, p. 596).

I join my friend I mentioned at the beginning; I, too, am glad to be a part of Laodicea. My desire is to open the door and let Jesus come in so that we can enjoy sweet fellowship together. I choose to add to the light of Laodicea's lamp, to work for the uplifting and reformation of God's last-day church.

In the next chapter, we will investigate more fully the other last-day church—the one called Babylon.

Discussion Questions:

1. Do you think most Adventists today have accepted the facts about Laodicea as presented in this chapter and no longer hold negative feelings about belonging to the church of Laodicea?
2. Why do you think every church except Laodicea receives some word of commendation? As you think back through the history of the Seventh-day Adventist church, do you conclude that we are *that*

bad? Worse even than Pergamos and Thyatira, those compromising and persecuting churches?
3. Ellen White says "the Laodicean message is full of encouragement." Where in that message do you find encouragement?
4. Ellen White also makes a clear distinction between Laodicea and Babylon. Why do you think that throughout the history of the Adventist church some have insisted on merging those identities?

Endnotes

1 Arthur L.White, *Ellen G. White: The Early Years* (Washington, D.C.: Review and Herald Publishing Assn., 1985), 342
2 C. Mervyn Maxwell, *God Cares* (Boise, Idaho: Pacific Press Publishing Assn., 1985), vol. 2, p. 98.

Chapter Five

THE FORGOTTEN ANGEL

> *"And another angel followed, saying, 'Babylon is fallen, is fallen, that great city, because she has made all nations drink of the wine of the wrath of her fornication.... And I heard another voice saying, 'Come out of her my people, lest you share in her sins, and lest you receive of her plagues'"* (Revelation 14:8; 18:4).

The literal city of Babylon was a desolate ruin the day John penned those words. Just as Jeremiah had prophesied, the day came when the glory of the Chaldean empire was not "inhabited but . . . wholly desolate" (Jeremiah 50:13). Founded by Nimrod, Babylon became a symbol of disbelief in the true God, its tower a monument to apostasy, its walls encircling a citadel of rebellion. The Bible carries that symbolism down the centuries to the end time when spiritual Babylon arises to "reign over the kings of the earth" (Revelation 17:18). And for her, as with her predecessor, the announcement will once again resound throughout the earth, "Babylon the great is fallen, is fallen" (Revelation 18:2)!

The prophet Isaiah identifies Lucifer as the invisible king of Babylon (Isaiah 14:4). Satan no doubt designed to make Babylon the capital of his kingdom and a base from which to secure control of the entire human race, just as God purposed to make Jerusalem the center of His efforts for man's salvation. Today those ancient cities still serve as symbols of the two great forces being gathered and energized to fight earth's final war.

Modern Babylon's identity

At least from the time of the Reformation, Protestants had identified spiritual Babylon as the papacy. But in the summer of 1843, one of the best-loved Millerite preachers, Charles Fitch, wrote a stirring article in *The Midnight Cry* in which he put the Babylon label on every church in the entire Christian world that opposed the plain teachings of Scripture.[1] This was a shockingly new idea to those in the Protestant churches. In time other Millerite preachers came to agree with Fitch, and the first call to come out of Babylon became a part of the message to prepare to meet Jesus in 1843-44.

Fitch was right. Babylon is not only "the great harlot" (Revelation 17:1), she is "the mother of harlots" (verse 5) who bears in her hand a golden cup filled with "the filthiness of her fornication" (verse 4). It makes sense that if a woman is the Bible's prophetic symbol for a church, then an adulterous woman represents *any* church that has willingly permitted its doctrinal positions to be dictated by Satan rather than by the Word of God. Those Protestant churches that, from the time of their rejection of the Loud Cry of 1843-44, have continued to reject the light of Bible truth, have voluntarily placed themselves among the great harlot's daughters and therefore qualify to be included as a part of Babylon.

Adventist pioneer J. N. Andrews, more than a hundred years ago, saw the tower-of-Babel phenomenon being repeated in Christian churches: "Since the great apostasy, the majority of his [Christ's] followers have busied themselves in attempting to climb up to heaven some other way. They have been confounded in the attempt, and scattered abroad upon the face of the earth, with creeds as discordant as the languages of those who were dispersed at the ancient tower."[2]

Babylon's sins

Revelation 18:5 says that Babylon's "sins have reached to heaven," and that she "has become a dwelling place of demons, a prison for every foul spirit, and a cage for every unclean and hated bird" (verse 2)! Notice how inclusive the language is: *"every* foul spirit, *"every* unclean bird." Demons have authored Babylon's theology. Every truth has been corrupted; every Bible doctrine turned into a lie. Babylon is rapidly approaching that time in her history when she has no redeeming qualities. Ellen White says, "A terrible condition of the religious world is here described" (*The Great Controversy*, p. 603).

The expression, "Babylon is fallen," has to apply to religious bodies that were once standing upright. "At the time of their rise these [Protestant Reformation] churches took a noble stand for God and the truth, and His blessing was with them. . . . But they fell by the same desire which was the curse and ruin of Israel—the desire of imitating the practices and courting the friendship of the ungodly" (*The Great Controversy*, p. 383).

The forces that derailed the Reformation churches have been numerous and powerful. Their failure to separate completely from the errors of Rome eventually wrecked havoc to their commitment to the centrality of Scripture. That, in turn, left them vulnerable to the so-called secular religions—rationalism, evolution, philosophy, materialism, humanism. They came to believe that these could be trusted to advance the well-being of mankind in practical ways that the God of the Bible seemed to be neglecting. They turned away from the Bible to the laboratory, the classroom, and the political arena in search of answers to human problems. Church leaders, rather than stemming the tide, either stood by helplessly while the juggernaut of infidelity rolled through their congregations and their institutions, or, in some cases, they themselves led the way into apostasy.

The result is that today it seems as if the last place people go to find out what is right and wrong is the church. Church leaders are strangely silent in the face of widespread moral chaos. While crime, divorce, drug use, pornography, teen suicides, and illegitimate births steadily increase, these leaders manifest more interest in politics, feminism, the environment, and the rights of homosexuals.

Many laypeople in the mainline churches over the last hundred years would have said that the move away from the authority of Scripture was not their idea. How is it, then, that conservative laypeople can end up with liberal leaders? Thomas Reeves, an Episcopalian historian, says this: "There is an important principle of group dynamics involved here: moderate, otherwise busy people are no match for zealous, ideological interest groups eager to attain power. . . . Conservatives tend to stay out of the political side of church life and concentrate on spreading the gospel. The inevitable result is a liberal takeover of church authority."[3]

The big torpedo that sank the mainline churches was higher criticism, itself a stepchild of the secular religions. Professors of theology came to look upon themselves more as scientific sleuths whose task was to outdo each other in discrediting the Bible. They have dissected every word, challenged the historical accuracy of every narrative, questioned the date and authorship of every book, and denied the reality of every miracle, including the incarnation and resurrection of Jesus.

The pastors trained under those professors went out to proclaim a social gospel that championed the cause of the homeless, minorities, women, gays, and criminals, but were unclear when it came to defining sin and the terms of salvation. They began to preach the God who loves unconditionally and judges each person by his or her own value system. Counseling, psychology, sociology, and political science crowded out a deep searching for biblical truth. Pastors caught up in the tidal wave of the social gospel have been described as believing anything, provided it's not in Holy Scripture.

If there is an upside to all of this, it is this: millions of the unfed parishioners in these churches are starving for the Bread of Life. Many of them would welcome a place of fellowship where the Bible is still meaningful. God's remnant church must be that place.

Listen to what Ellen White says on that very point: "Not a few are dissatisfied with their present condition and are longing for clearer light. They look in vain for the image of Christ in the churches with which they are connected. As these bodies depart further and further from the truth, and ally themselves more closely with the world, the difference between the two classes will widen, and it will finally result in separation. The time will come when those who love God supremely can no longer remain in connection with such as are 'lovers of pleasures more than lovers of God; having a form of godliness, but denying the power thereof'" (*The Great Controversy*, p. 390).

Whatever we might say about Adventist lifestyles, we can say without hesitation that the distance between Babylon and the beliefs of the Seventh-day Adventist church is enormous. The Sabbath, the state of the dead, the sanctuary ministry of Jesus, the Second Coming and millenium, spiritual gifts, healthful living—these are the points of difference we usually cite. But where is *any* common ground?

For instance, ask any Christian outside of Adventism why Christ had to die, and they will probably say, "He died to save me from my sins." But if asked about the obligation to keep the Ten Commandments, the same person will most likely say that Christ's death also annulled the law.

Wine is intoxicating. Wine destroys one's power of reason. The mind confused by the wine of Babylon somehow cannot follow simple logic: if there is no law, there is no sin; and if there is no sin, Christ's death was a foolish waste. God is dethroned. He is denied the right to decide what moral imperatives should govern the universe. He is no longer the Sovereign Lord. It is that kind of confusion on something so basic to the heart and soul of the Christian religion that warrants the label Babylon.

Years ago the mainline churches of America were looked upon as constituting the moral backbone of this nation. Their pastors set the moral tone in their communities, and state and national leaders sought their counsel. Today, American presidents and statesmen are about as likely to take counsel with the Catholic pope as they are with the leaders of Protestant churches, probably because the pope comes across as self-assured, while they appear vacillating and confused.

These church leaders may take a strong position against abortion but say little or nothing about pre-marital sex. They may object to drugs but not to alcohol. They are both pro family and pro gay rights. They profess to rely on the power of the Holy Spirit yet are deeply involved in politics, even seeking for civil power to enforce their religious views. They may occasionally preach against worldliness yet virtually every survey shows no difference between the way they and their secular counterparts entertain themselves. The same can be said of divorce rates, spousal abuse, and child molestation.

This confusion has led to a steady drift away from anything that could be defined as moral absolutes, leaving these church leaders and their congregations with no rock-bottom form or substance to their theology. According to Dinesh D'Souza, such ambivalence has led great numbers of nominal Christians to confess, "We want to be saved as long as we are not saved from our sins. We are quite willing to be saved from a whole host of social evils, from poverty to disease to war. But we want to leave untouched the personal evils, such as selfishness and lechery and pride. We need spiritual healing, but we do not want it."[4]

Babylon's future

Many of the references to Babylon in the Old Testament picture her as the enemy of God's people. While God used her as an instrument to sometimes punish His people, in the end, Babylon, a cruel and idolatrous nation, will be utterly destroyed (Jeremiah 51:6-9). In the

New Testament, spiritual Babylon is also the great persecutor of God's true followers throughout the Christian era. And while she will wield great power over the entire world in the end time, her total destruction is forecast. "And great Babylon was remembered before God, to give her the cup of the wine of the fierceness of His wrath" (Revelation 16:19). "With violence the great city Babylon shall be thrown down, and shall not be found anymore" because "in her was found the blood of prophets and saints, and of all who were slain on the earth" (Revelation 18:21, 24).

How does Laodicea relate to Babylon?

Strange as it may seem, almost from its founding, some professed Seventh-day Adventists have decided that the church has also become Babylon and have tried to use that as cause for calling people out to start a new movement. If the English language has meaning, the question of the Adventist church being Babylon has been settled beyond all controversy.

"To claim that the Seventh-day Adventist Church is Babylon, is to make the same claim as does Satan . . . My brother, if you are teaching that the Seventh-day Adventist church is Babylon, you are wrong. God has not given you any such message to bear. . . . We are not to think that the chosen ones of God who are trying to walk in the light compose Babylon. The fallen denominational churches are Babylon" (*Testimonies to Ministers and Gospel Workers*, pp. 42, 59, 61).

So we can conclude that the organized Seventh-day Adventist denomination has never been, is not now, and never will be a part of Babylon—some members, yes; some leaders, maybe; some entire congregations, perhaps. Satan is certainly trying to convince as many of us as he can that it is possible to hold citizenship in both Zion and Babylon.

We must be sure we remember that great numbers of God's people are still in Babylon. Today, Babylon is the target of the most intense evangelistic outreach in the history of the world. "After these things I saw another angel coming down from heaven, having great authority, and the earth was illuminated with his glory. And he cried mightily with a loud voice, saying, 'Babylon the great is fallen, is fallen . . .' And I heard another voice from heaven saying, 'Come out of her, my people'" (Revelation 18:1, 2, 4).

Speaking of this same massive outreach movement, Ellen White writes, "Servants of God, with their faces lighted up and shining with holy consecration, will hasten from place to place to proclaim the message from heaven. By thousands of voices, all over the earth, the warning will be given" (*The Great Controversy*, p. 612).

Those voices are the voices of Laodiceans who have opened their hearts and let Jesus fully come into their lives. Now they are driven by a deep love for souls to give the "most solemn warning ever given to man" ("Thoroughness in Christian Work," *Review and Herald*, January 27, 1885). Those voices, of course, include the voices of Adventist publishing houses, radio stations, television studios, and educational and medical institutions.

Laodicea must give the three angels' messages to Babylon but be guarded against any alliances or association with Babylon that would compromise that mission. Today there is a keen interest in building bridges to connect the three parts that compose the city of Babylon—Catholicism, apostate Protestantism, and spiritualism (Revelation 16:13; 19). The 1994 document "Evangelicals and Catholics Together" was signed by Catholic bishops and such Protestant luminaries as Charles Colson, J. I. Packer, and Max Lucado. Then on October 31, 1999, Lutheran and Catholic leaders signed the "Joint Declaration on the Doctrine of Justification." Methodists officially signed the latter on July 23, 2006.

Many Seventh-day Adventists see this as a remarkable fulfillment of prophecy (Revelation 13:1-10); however, some may not be aware that we are doing some bridge building ourselves. We have already cited how the message and mission of the mainline denominations were derailed by educating their pastors in universities that did not share their goals. Yet many of our pulpits are occupied today by pastors who have been educated in those same universities and who have gone to Babylon's mega-churches to learn about church growth. I believe the overall impact on our mission has been negative.

We have been strictly warned not to compromise or blur our denominational identity. "At this time, when we are so near the end, shall we become so like the world in practice that men may look in vain to find God's denominated people? Shall any man sell our peculiar characteristics as God's chosen people for any advantage the world has to give? Shall the favor of those who transgress the law of God be looked upon as of great value? Shall those whom the Lord has named His people suppose that there is any power higher than the great I AM? Shall we endeavor to blot out the distinguishing points of faith that have made us Seventh-day Adventists?" (*Evangelism*, p. 121).

The forgotten angel

From the earliest days of our history, the preaching of the three angels' messages of Revelation 14 has defined the Seventh-day Adventist mission. In fact, we have seen that task as justifying our very existence. We know them by heart. The first angel announces the judgment; the second, the fall of Babylon; the third, the dire consequences of receiving the mark of the beast.

Our pastors and evangelists, for the most part, are faithfully preaching the first and third angels' messages. But I hear a somewhat muted trumpet when the second angel is asked to sound. Why is that message quite faithfully applied to the papacy but less often to apostate Protestantism? It is true that every time a sermon, book, or magazine article presents *any* aspect of the Adventist message, it calls attention, at least in an indirect way, to the errors of Babylon. But we seem to be holding back more than we should from presenting the message of the second angel clearly and forcefully when we have such plain counsel from the inspired pen of Ellen White: "The Protestants of the United States will be foremost in stretching their hands across the gulf to grasp the hand of spiritualism; they will reach over the abyss to clasp hands with the Roman power; and under the influence of this threefold union, this country will follow in the steps of Rome in trampling on the rights of conscience" (*The Great Controversy*, p. 588)

I think we hold back for the following reasons:

1. We are afraid of weakening our influence with other churches. Warnings against that mentality have been around for a long time. In 1973, Kenneth Wood, editor of the *Review and Herald*, wrote, "Too often, they [our members] try to minimize the differences between the Adventist church and other churches, and between the Adventist Church and the world."[5]

We certainly ought to love all people sincerely and unselfishly as Christ has commanded. But the second angel's message is designed to keep us from becoming more ecumenical than we should be. While Babylon continues its free fall into the abyss of error, I fear many Seventh-day Adventists have the idea that the distance between them and us is actually *shrinking*. We are setting aside the Bible and Spirit of Prophecy counsel and bringing in (or going to) non-Adventists to teach us how to worship, how to do soul-winning, how to rear our children and save our marriages, how to make our churches grow, etc. We need to trust God and seek the abundant counsel He has given, rather than go to the gods of Ekron for the healing of Adventism.

2. We fear being seen as judgmental. We live in a climate of openness and acceptance—not just acceptance of individuals but acceptance of wholly contradictory viewpoints. Our inclusiveness may be making us more pluralistic than we realize. We have heard the gospel of tolerance for so long that we may have come to really believe there is more than one way to heaven.

We fear that being too explicit about the false teachings of other churches will slow the growth of our own.

And so we open the door wider and wider. Columnist George Will speaks to that point with this insightful observation: "If a nation or institution is limitlessly inclusive, then citizenship or membership is meaningless."[6]

"The message we have to bear is not a message that men need to cringe to declare. They are not to seek to cover it, to conceal its origin and purpose. Its advocates must be men who will not hold their peace day nor night" (*Life Sketches of Ellen G. White*, p. 329).

"Men of faith and prayer will be constrained to go forth with holy zeal, declaring the words which God gives them. The sins of Babylon will be laid open. . . . Thousands upon thousands will listen who have never heard words like these. In amazement they hear the testimony that Babylon is the church, fallen because of her errors and sins . . ." (*The Great Controversy*, pp. 606, 607).

The foregoing counsel is designed to make us faithful in the fulfillment of our task; it is not a license for church bashing. We must heed the following admonition as well: "God has jewels in all the churches, and it is not for us to make sweeping denunciations of the professed religious world" (*Last Day Events*, p. 197).

But at least the warning should be given with great clarity to our own people. Certainly *they* should be warned away from following Babylon over the precipice—from letting her culture, rather than the Bible, dictate our values; from sitting by quietly while the liberalizing element takes charge; from letting the insidious poison of compromise erode away the purity of our faith. The churches which are becoming Babylon and which will one day receive the terrible outpouring of God's wrath are becoming that way largely because of the silence of good people. And that is the danger for us.

3. We are afraid of the cult label. We want to be seen as a regular church—to minimize our differences and maximize our similarities. "The Remnant is distinctive," writes Laurel Damsteegt, "but we are getting uneasy with this differentiation. . . . To remember who Babylon is has become uncomfortable to us today. . . . Meanwhile Babylon infiltrates us. . . . We must remember who we are, or we have no reason to be."[7]

4. We are afraid to give correction and reproof to others when doing so might call attention to our own shortcomings. We fear to say what we are commissioned to say about Babylon because of what it also says about us. If we are pandering to those who want entertainment in the place of reverent worship; if we show hostility toward pastors who preach the straight testimony of the Word; if our divorce rate, drug use, and teenage pregnancy are little different from other denominations, or even the secular world, we are ourselves taking sips from the cup which the harlot of Revelation 17 holds to our lips.

God's mercy toward those still in Babylon

Even though the second angel's message was first preached (and rejected) in the summer of 1844, in the end of time, a final opportunity will be given, "and the people of God still in Babylon will be called upon to separate from her communion. This message is the last that will ever be given to the world; and it will accomplish its work" (*The Great Controversy*, p. 390).

Right now we have three groups—the faithful, the uninformed, and the rejecters—existing side by side. As we near the end of the period of Laodicea, however, everyone will hear the message and receive the invitation to separate from Babylon. Revelation 18:1 says, "The earth was illuminated with his glory." That light will cause the unenlightened group to disappear. Only the receivers and the rejecters remain.

We are even now experiencing the fulfillment of that prophecy. We are receiving into our churches a great harvest of souls from other churches, as well as from the non-Christian world. The thousands that are flocking to Adventist churches in Inter-America, Russia, South America, India, and Africa will come to us in North America, too, when we are ready. "Multitudes will receive the faith and join the armies of the Lord" (*Evangelism*, p. 700). "Thousands in the eleventh hour will see and acknowledge the truth. . . . These conversions to truth will be made with a rapidity that will surprise the church, and God's name alone will be glorified" (*Selected Messages*, bk. 2, p.16).

May it be soon!

In the next chapter, we will tackle the troublesome question of apostasy.

Discussion Questions:

1. What would you say are the specific sins of Babylon that should be most forcefully proclaimed and warned against? Or is this not the time?
2. How can the second angel's message be given with clarity and yet with tact? If you were to prepare a sermon or write an article, how would you do that?
3. Which of the five reasons given for our reluctance to be more forceful in our exposure of the erroneous teachings of the Protestant churches do you think predominates?
4. Of all the forces that eventually made the churches of the Reformation guilty of the sins of Babylon, which do you think is operating most effectively to do the same within Adventism?
5. Although not discussed in this chapter, spiritualism (which takes in all the non-Christian religions of Eastern mysticism) is a part of Babylon. How do we tailor our call to "come out of Babylon" to their world view?

Endnotes

1. Arthur Whitefield Spalding, *Origin and History of Seventh-day Adventists* (Washington, D.C.: Review and Herald Publishing Association., 1961), 175.
2. J. N. Andrews, *Three Messages of Revelation 14* (Hagerstown: Review and Herald Publishing Association., 1892) 48.
3. Thomas Reeves, *The Empty Church* (New York: The Free Press, 1989), 15.
4. Dinesh D'Souza, *What's So Great About Christianity?*

(Washington, D.C.: Regnery Publishing, Inc., 2007), 272.
5   Kenneth H. Wood, *Review and Herald* (June 21, 1973).
6   George Will, *Newsweek* (November 10, 2003): 74.
7   Laurel Damsteegt, "The Remnant's Vision: Getting Foggy?" *Adventists Affirm* (Fall 1988): 21-23.

Chapter Six

THE APOSTASY QUESTION

> *"Also from among yourselves men will rise up, speaking perverse things, to draw away the disciples after themselves. Therefore watch"* (Acts 20:30, 31)

> *"In latter times some will depart from the faith, giving heed to deceiving spirits and doctrines of demons, speaking lies in hypocrisy"* (1 Timothy 4:1, 2)

Is the Seventh-day Adventist church in apostasy? That question is sure to ignite a heated, polarizing debate. Many of those who answer "yes" are joining various dissident groups; those who answer "no" may stay by the church but be unhappy with its spiritual condition.

Is it correct to say that the *church* is in apostasy? Or is it more correct to say that *apostasy* is in the church? What criteria determine the answers to those questions? Let's investigate four possibilities.

1. Apostasy is measured by <u>how many</u> in the church are in a rebellious or careless and back-slidden state. Available data could easily be interpreted to support that conclusion. On average, less than half of the members in the North American Division attend church regularly. In addition, it is likely that even among regular attendees some are lax in Sabbath-keeping, are stealing the tithe, and have virtually nothing in the way of a devotional life. Too many are much more enamored with sports and movies than they are with soul-winning. Their attachment to the world is attested to by immodest dress, jewelry, and bad health practices.

The problem with the numbers answer is this: until persecution and other sifting agencies have done their work, we can't be sure how many from the non-attendees

The Apostasy Question

will be restored to faith and how many now attending will abandon ship or be converted. It is virtually futile to try to measure the present spirituality of our fellow church members, much less their future commitment. We can observe bad behavior, but we cannot measure motive. Surely, if in the crisis ahead "many a star we have admired for its brilliance will then go out in darkness" (*Prophets and Kings*, p. 188) how are we to measure the spirituality of lesser lights? Elijah's guess was off by 700,000 percent!

Another huge problem that confronts those trying to do a head count of the sheep and the goats is that they can make only so many personal observations. It is obviously foolish for someone in Oregon to attempt to measure the spirituality of members in Wisconsin, much less those in Ghana, Chile, or Taiwan.

I am reminded of a veteran worker's comment at a teacher's convention in Idaho many years ago. He was introduced as coming from Southern California. He began by acknowledging that (in those days) "Californian Adventists" carried certain negative connotations, and then he said this: "I have traveled back and forth across the North American continent and to some extent around the world, and I have concluded that the saints are pretty evenly distributed."

So we eventually have to circle back and face the fact that our energies are best employed in addressing the spirituality of ourselves and our own congregation and leave the numbering of Israel to God.

2. Apostasy is measured by the <u>level</u> of apostasy—that is, by the heinousness of the sins being committed. Seventh-day Adventists should certainly be alarmed as they see their fellow believers becoming more and more familiar with the grosser forms of sin. Rampant Sabbath-breaking, gluttony, fornication, spousal abuse, child molestation—these are levels of apostasy that should greatly distress us all. Solomon drifted downward from marrying idolatrous wives, to gross dissipation, to offering his children to Molech—the most monstrous of crimes. And even from that point on, Israel was described as sinking "lower and still lower in apostasy" (*Prophets and Kings*, p. 281).

But how do we measure *our* condition on a "low-lower-lowest" scale? We are told that "the least deviation from right and principle will lead to separation from God and may end in apostasy" (*Testimonies for the Church*, vol. 4, p. 578); and that "the work of apostasy begins in some secret rebellion of the heart against the requirements of God's law" (*God's Amazing Grace*, p. 333).

Prophecy tells us to expect big surprises ahead. What we thought were "rich floors of wheat" will turn out to be "chaff blown away with the fan of God" (*Maranatha*, p. 204). It would be natural to expect those who continually find fault with their fellow members to eventually forsake the church. And we certainly won't be counting on the fidelity of those who are immoral and dishonest. But we may be thrown into a state of shock by the departure of those whom we now view as pillars.

Measuring the *depth* of apostasy in the church is also complicated by the tendency of our own values to shift over time, causing us to measure with a different yardstick today than we did yesterday. The relentless pressure of the popular culture is surely shaping most of us more than we realize. What is viewed as strict or high standard today might have been considered permissive fifty or sixty years ago. If God were to subject all of us to a letter-of-the-law, Bible-and-Spirit-of-Prophecy examination of our thinking and conduct, where would we fall on the faith-apostasy scale?

3. Apostasy is measured by the spirituality of church leaders. That seems fair enough. At least the *numbers* are greatly reduced! Instead of 16 million members to monitor, we now have something like 25,000 pastors, administrators, and departmental workers to evaluate.

And now we also have some fairly objective criteria to work with. We can test our pastor's preaching and lifestyle by biblical standards. We can evaluate the spiritual tenor and doctrinal integrity of the church's publications.

The Apostasy Question

We can listen to Adventist radio and watch Adventist television and give those our ratings. We can attend conference constituency meetings and camp meetings and observe our local conference leaders in action.

Old Testament history would seem to encourage us to measure apostasy in the church by the spirituality of its leaders. If Israel's kings were faithful and reform-minded (Asa, Hezekiah, and Josiah), Israel seemed to prosper; but if they "did evil in the sight of the Lord" (Ahab, Jehoram, and Manasseh), Israel languished. There was apparently little accountability for the rank and file of the citizens; the spirituality of the king and his courtiers was the measure of the nation.

Before we go forth with our measuring rod, however, we need to remember that church leadership can be incredibly difficult. Leaders may make some errors so blatant as to seem wholly inexcusable, but I believe most of them really want to do the right thing—not only the right thing, but the wisest thing. While some of us might be inclined to go with a pre-emptive strike against wrong-doing, a particular church leader may choose to pursue the more patient path of revival and reformation. Remember, too, that the low spirituality of their constituents may, to a large degree, serve to put an otherwise consecrated leader in chains.

We will discuss how to protest the wrongs in the church in the next chapter; right now let's remind ourselves that we can make a difference in our local church by helping to elect and support leaders who are dedicated to taking the church on an upward course.

4. Apostasy is measured by how individuals or the church relate to adopted doctrinal positions. I believe we have now arrived on safer ground. The dictionary says apostasy is an abandonment of what one has formerly believed. In other words, apostasy is not just *behaving* contrary to one's profession; it is the clear *repudiation* of beliefs once held. It announces a loss of faith, or a change of faith. It usually leads to the severing of one's attachment to a church or movement (or being asked to leave).

59

Let's take that as a working definition and walk through the apostasy question at the individual, congregational, conference, and denominational level.

The individual

We would probably charge a fellow church member with being in apostasy if he or she were to commit adultery. But there are two kinds of adulterers: those who are remorseful and repentant, and those who are convinced that their relationship is heaven-approved. Are both in apostasy? Not if we apply the definition we have just adopted.

Everyone struggles with certain temptations as they strive to grow daily in Christ. So, again, we conclude it isn't *conduct alone* that makes a person an apostate; it is a change in the way they formerly believed or professed to believe, regarding God and spiritual values. Breaking God's law may or may not be defined as apostasy, but *believing that lawbreaking is okay* certainly qualifies. Apostates not only disobey God's law, but they deny the validity of the requirement itself and defend their conduct as above reproach.

"Some shall depart from the faith, giving heed to seducing spirits and doctrines of devils" (1 Timothy 4:1, KJV). "And they will turn their ears away from the truth, and be turned aside to fables" (2 Timothy 4:4). They depart from the faith because the adoption of the doctrines of devils has given them a whole new way of believing. They consciously and deliberately "turn their ears away from the truth," because they have found fables which accord with their beliefs and lifestyle. Bible truth is no longer palatable to them. As they settle into these new doctrinal positions, they become less and less inclined to receive counsel and correction. It doesn't mean they can never be re-converted and restored to a life of faith, but right now they are in apostasy. Apostasy enters the church one person at a time.

The Apostasy Question

The local church

In like manner, a local church can be said to be in apostasy, not just because some of its members are in clear violation of biblical lifestyle standards, but because that congregation rejects and/or seeks to change what the church at large believes and teaches. Let's say a majority of members in a local congregation voted to serve alcoholic beverages at their fellowship meals. That church could be said to be in apostasy and could no longer justly lay claim to its Adventist identity.

The local conference

The same would be true of a local conference. If the majority of the delegates attending a duly-called conference business session voted that henceforth their official position would be to deny any validity to the claim of inspiration for Ellen White, that conference could be said to be in apostasy.

The General Conference

And finally, let's suppose the majority of the delegates to a General Conference quinquennial session voted that homosexual practices were no longer to be considered immoral and cause for church discipline. The Seventh-day Adventist denomination could rightfully be charged with apostasy and considered a part of Babylon. Until something of that nature happens, we need to be slow to charge the Seventh-day Adventist church *as a denomination* with being in apostasy.

I have been asked if any and all departures from the faith that qualify as apostasy, other than at the personal level, must be *by vote*. My answer is no. A specific doctrinal position can be set aside by common consent as well as by vote. In fact, I am convinced that this is the way change usually happens. I know of churches where basic Adventist beliefs are commonly ignored, and where there seems to be an understanding among the members that these matters will not be made an issue. So, following our working definition, such churches can be said to be in apostasy.

My point in the foregoing discussion has been to establish a way of measuring apostasy that is reasonably free of subjective measures. I conclude that when the truth is set aside by vote, we have an objective criterion. If the same result is obtained by consensus, that doesn't change the conclusion.

Israel's Apostasy

I believe God's dealing with Israel illustrates the concept that it is *truth* that ultimately measures what is or is not apostasy. Throughout the Old Testament, God is pictured as patiently entreating His people to come into a closer relationship with Him. One of the most touching is found in Isaiah 65:2: "I have stretched out My hands all day long to a rebellious people, who walk in a way that is not good." The vineyard parable in the fifth chapter of Isaiah also pictures God's great love for His people. He bestows tender care on the vineyard (Israel), but instead of fine table grapes, it produces inedible wild grapes.

But the Old Testament also contains repeated warnings that there are limits to divine forbearance, that there is the real possibility that God could sever His relationship with His professed people. The time comes when the Great Vine-dresser says, "Now, please let Me tell you what I will do to My vineyard: I will take away its hedge, and it shall be burned . . . I will lay it waste" (Isaiah 5:5, 6).

As we look back through centuries of stiff-necked rebellion, through endless cycles of backsliding and reform, we marvel at God's forbearance. After all, what could be worse than priests having sexual affairs with women worshippers? Or parents sacrificing their children on pagan altars? Or kings ordering the execution of prophets? Why would God put up with such ugly behavior? The answer, I believe is found in Paul's affirmation that to Israel were given "the oracles of God" (Romans 3:2).

The Apostasy Question

These words have profound meaning. Israel was God's designated, denominated people, not because they were perfect, but because He had given them the truth. Israel was the place to find the truth about God. It was found in the witness of a Jewish servant girl in the household of Naaman and a boy named Joseph in the household of Potiphar. And even though it was not always lived out in the lives of Israelites, it was inscribed on the parchment rolls of the prophets and proclaimed in synagogue and sanctuary. If one were to find the true God anywhere in that otherwise pagan world, it was in the temple services at Jerusalem and in the inspired messages of Israel's seers.

And God's church holds the same position in the world today. If one is looking for truth—not perfect behavior, but *truth*—there is only one place in the world where it can be found. "God has called His church in this day, *as He called ancient Israel*, to stand as a light in the earth. By the mighty cleaver of truth, the messages of the first, second, and third angels, He has separated them from the churches and from the world to bring them into a sacred nearness to Himself. He has made them *the depositaries of His law* and has committed to them the great truths of prophecy for this time. Like the holy oracles committed to ancient Israel, these are a sacred trust to be communicated to the world" (*Testimonies for the Church*, vol. 5, pp. 455, 456).

Note that Ellen White makes a direct comparison between Israel and the Seventh-day Adventist church as the guardians of truth. Notice, also, the word "depositaries," a word we've seen before. The truth has been *deposited* with the church. If anyone in the world knows the truths encompassed by the three angels' messages, those truths were most likely communicated to them by some person, publication, or agency of the Seventh-day Adventist church. That truth, which qualifies as "present truth," has no other source, unless it were to be given to someone by an angel or by special revelation.

So *truth* is the issue that ultimately decides the apostasy question. Babylon is Babylon, not only because its members behave more unseemly than the members of the remnant, but because they have over and over again taken positions that stand clearly against Scripture. Clifford Goldstein makes the point: "It is ultimately truth, not holiness, that distinguishes God's *corporate* remnant people today just as it did in the days of ancient Israel."[1]

If one belongs to a church that has the truth, there is always the possibility that, by God's grace, he will bring his life into conformity with that truth. On the other hand, if the church to which he belongs denies the validity of Bible truth and rejects its applicability to life, his hope for finding the path to heaven through *that* church is not likely, and probably non-existent. We conclude, then, that while there is apostasy in the Seventh-day Adventist church, if one measures the church by its official relationship to truth, it cannot now be said to be in apostasy.

But what if we were to follow the Israel-Adventist parallel all the way through? After all, the 490 years of Israel's probation, as prophesied in Daniel 9:24, did end. Could not the Seventh-day Adventist church be wearing out the patience of God and facing the end of its period of probation? I believe there is a good answer to that question.

Our time of visitation

Jesus spoke of His time among His people as the "time of your visitation" (Luke 19:44). Bible prophets had used the metaphor before to designate a time when a final, testing truth comes to a nation, the world, or the church that separates those who are loyal to God from those who have chosen the path of rebellion (see Isaiah 10:3; Jeremiah 10:15). The time of visitation is a time when the Holy Spirit visits people with truth before they are visited with divine judgment. The times and the messages given before the Flood, before the destruction of Sodom, before the Babylonian captivity, and before the destruction of Jerusalem serve as examples.

So is there a "time of visitation" for the world and the church today? Yes. "Jesus, looking down to the last

The Apostasy Question

generation, saw the world involved in a deception similar to that which caused the destruction of Jerusalem. The great sin of the Jews was their rejection of Christ; the great sin of the Christian world would be their rejection of the law of God, the foundation of His government in heaven and earth. . . . Millions in bondage to sin, slaves of Satan, doomed to suffer the second death, would refuse to listen to the words of truth *in their day of visitation.* Terrible blindness! strange infatuation!" (*The Great Controversy*, pp. 22, 23).

The Jews rejected Christ; our generation is rejecting God's law. It's a strange switch. They did not recognize their need of grace; today the Christian world in general does not recognize how necessary to their salvation obedience to God's law is. "Everyone who does evil is good in the sight of the Lord, and He delights in them" (Malachi 2:17); that is the comforting message that has gone out to the inhabitants of our world. This is the major heresy of apostate Christianity, and it has, to some degree, infiltrated Seventh-day Adventist churches.

It is interesting that Ellen White referred to the Holy Spirit as the "heavenly Visitant" (*Testimonies for the Church*, vol. 8, p. 62). In our day of visitation, it is so very crucial that we recognize and accept His sanctifying ministry in our lives. Israel's legalism led it to reject the *Great Justifier* of God's people. A brand of "righteousness by faith" popular among Seventh-day Adventists today is leading us to reject the *Great Sanctifier* of God's people.

Now, while we should learn from Israel's experience, we must realize that we are coming to a point in earth's history when such comparisons with the past must end. The faith-apostasy cycle must end. Laodicea, as we have pointed out, is the last of the seven churches. Raising up an eighth church is not God's answer to the apostasy question. The closing up of earth's history calls for a different solution. This time the church is to be purified, not disowned. Instead of the Seventh-day Adventist church rejecting the truths committed to it, those very truths will eventually be the sieve through which God separates the wheat from the chaff.

The day of Israel's visitation closed with God's rejection of them as His denominated people and the establishment of the Christian church. The day of our visitation will close with the sifting and sealing of God's people, the Latter Rain, the Loud Cry, and the Second Coming. Those who have sinned against the Holy Spirit will leave the church in droves, making room for the truly converted to take their places.

"We shall have apostasies; we expect them. 'They will go out from us because they were not of us' (see 1 John 2:19)" (*Selected Messages*, bk. 3, p. 425). "Frequent will be the apostasies of men who have occupied responsible positions" (*Last Day Events*, p. 179). "Said the angel, 'Rebellion will occur up to the time of the closing up of the work of the third angel's message. Marvel not, neither be discouraged. He who conquered the leader in rebellion stands at the head of this great work. . . . Rebels will be purged out from among the loyal and true in due time, for the truth has gathered of every kind'" (*Manuscript Releases*, vol. 5, p. 297).

But will these apostasies, even of prominent leaders, decimate our numbers and leave the church in shambles? No! "There are men who will receive the truth, and these will take the places made vacant by those who become offended and leave the truth. . . . Men of true Christian principle will take their place, and will become faithful, trustworthy householders, to advocate the word of God in its true bearings, and in its simplicity. The Lord will work so that the disaffected ones will be separated from the true and loyal ones. . . . The ranks will not be diminished. Those who are firm and true will close up the vacancies that are made by those who become offended and apostatize" (*Maranatha*, p. 200).

This important truth cannot be overstated: The church will be brought to the brink and will "appear as if about to fall," but the organized church itself does not go into apostasy; the apostates leave the church.

The Apostasy Question

Let's turn to Nehemiah 9:20, 21. This passage does not, in any way, excuse the rampant backsliding in our beloved church, but it encourages the faithful to stay the course. "You also gave your good Spirit to instruct them, and did not withhold Your manna from their mouth, and gave them water for their thirst. Forty years You sustained them in the wilderness. They lacked nothing. Their clothes did not wear out and their feet did not swell."

They ate manna for forty years. Please do not let that slide past you. Think with me about a few things that were happening during those forty years.

Early on, when they first reached the borders of Canaan at Kadesh-Barnea, they openly rebelled and refused to enter, even electing a captain to lead them back to Egypt—and yet the manna kept falling.

At the foot of Mt. Sinai, in the very presence of the living God, apostate Israelites danced around a senseless idol—and yet, the next day little boys and girls were out gathering the manna for breakfast.

Then there was the terrible rebellion of Korah, Dathan, and Abiram that led to the deaths of thousands—and yet the survivors were baking manna cakes for dinner the next day.

Two of their chief priests, Nadab and Abihu, tried to enter the temple while intoxicated and were incinerated—and still the manna fell from heaven upon a grieving congregation.

At the borders of Canaan the second time, many, including church leaders, became involved with Moabite prostitutes, even bringing them right into the camp—yet even that did not stop the manna from falling.

And finally, Moses himself, their great spiritual leader, disobeyed God and struck the rock in a fit of anger. And that night, as silently as the dew forms on the grass, the manna fell again to feed the hungry multitudes—both the faithful and the unfaithful.

Three hundred sixty-five days a year, year after year, summer and winter, *for forty years*, the blessing came upon the church! Why? Because God loves His church

The Church That Does Not Fall

and does not withhold heaven's gifts from those who are faithful because the wayward and rebellious are in the camp. Let's learn from this that the right church can have bad leaders and unworthy members. So stay by the church! Are there problems in God's church today? Yes. A quick look in the mirror should help answer that question! But in spite of us, the work is going forward this very moment. One would have to be totally out of touch not to recognize the Holy Spirit's working in and through the church in these last days.

While some are busy finding fault, others are busy finding precious souls and bringing them to Christ.

While the church's critics broadcast their poison, Adventist World Radio, the Hope Channel, 3ABN, and others are broadcasting the three angels' messages to millions.

While some seem paralyzed with anger and discouragement because of the low spiritual level of the church, hundreds of thousands in India, Indonesia, and South America are breaking away from Satan's control, renouncing pagan customs, and preparing for the return of Jesus.

While the devil's moles are digging tunnels under the church's doctrinal foundations, ADRA is drilling wells and feeding the starving in Africa.

While some adults find pleasure in tearing down the church, consecrated youth are helping Maranatha Volunteers build hundreds of new churches around the world.

While false shepherds are allowing the sheep to be ravaged by wolves, thousands of faithful pastors and evangelists are repairing the breach, building up the hedge, and giving the trumpet a certain sound.

The manna keeps falling! The manna of the Holy Spirit continues to be poured out, and the work is going forward. Let me ask this: If you and I had been members of the wilderness church, how much manna would we have found outside the environs of the camp? None. The manna was not given to feed Ishmaelite camel drivers or Caananite hunters roving the Sinai Peninsula. The manna does not fall outside the camp! Neither will the

The Apostasy Question

latter rain come to those who are not at their post of duty *inside* the church. Do not listen to those who would try to convince you otherwise.

"There is no need to doubt, to be fearful that the work will not succeed. God is at the head of the work, and He will set everything in order. If matters need adjusting at the head of the work, God will attend to that, and work to right every wrong. Let us have faith that God is going to carry the noble ship which bears the people of God safely into port" (*Maranatha*, p. 129).

While the wheat and the tares grow together, our task is to be the most faithful members we can be. If apostasy enters the church one member at a time, so does victory and renewal. Just as each Israelite gathered his own portion of the manna, so each of us may receive our portion of the Holy Spirit and experience the new birth each day.

In the meantime, how much do we have to put up with? How do we protest the wrongs we see in the church?

Discussion Questions:

1. Which of the four measures of apostasy do you think most of our members use? Which one have you been using?
2. For what problems of disobedience among our members are church leaders accountable? And for which are the members of the local churches accountable?
3. Do you agree that ultimately it is the church's official relationship to truth that is the best measure of apostasy? If so, how important is it that we know the truth and do our part in maintaining its pre-eminence in the church?
4. Israel was eventually disowned and replaced with the Christian church. Why will the Seventh-day Adventist church, as a denomination, not be replaced?
5. Ellen White said, "We shall have apostasies; we expect them." And then she follows that with this quote from 1 John 2:19: "They will go out from us because they

were not of us." What does that last statement say about the survival of the church?

Endnotes

1   Clifford Goldstein, *The Remnant* (Boise: Pacific Press Publishing Association, 1994), 98.

Chapter Seven

HOW TO PROTEST THE WRONGS IN THE CHURCH

> *"Cry aloud, spare not; lift up your voice like a trumpet; tell My people their transgression, and the house of Jacob their sins" (Isaiah 58:1).*

Many conscientious church members are deeply troubled by the problems in the church today. They honestly do not know what to do. They may feel like the deep-sea diver who was busily at work on the ocean floor when suddenly, from 200-feet above, the captain's voice crackles in his ears: "Hurry! Get ready to come up on deck!"

"Why, what's the matter?" the diver asks.

"The ship is sinking!" the captain shouts back.

It is one thing to live and work in the dangerous environment of this world; however, it is devastating to be told that the one place above all that you have counted upon as your haven of refuge is sinking into apostasy.

The church has always had problems. Much of the Bible documents those problems, and many of the prophets were virtually full-time protesters. The church was so back-slidden in Ezekiel's time that he referred to it as the "sister of Sodom" (Ezekiel 16:49). Isaiah described the church in his time as "a people laden with iniquity" (Isaiah 1:4). Jesus referred to the church leaders of His day as hypocrites and a "brood of vipers" (Matthew 23:29, 33). Paul was appalled at the gross sins committed in the church at Corinth (1 Corinthians 5). Ellen White was forced to address virtually every sin known to man in the church of her day.

Plenty of publications, websites, and audio and video materials tell us about the church's problems today—pastors who have rejected the Spirit of Prophecy, rock-and-roll worship services, members who are attending sports events on the Sabbath, college Bible teachers who are promoting some unorthodox theology, etc. Our church members usually respond to the perceived wrongs in the church in one of four ways:

1. Vent their anger and disappointment on anyone who will listen. Following Matthew 18 is not a requirement they take seriously. Criticizing and complaining is their way of sighing and crying.

2. Try to ignore the problems. They may be troubled, but they decide to "go with the flow." They pretend not to see. They conclude that it is not their responsibility to confront the wayward ones. They decide the issue is not worth causing hard feelings and dividing the church. It may sound harsh, but Isaiah called such people "dumb dogs" that "cannot bark" (Isaiah 56:10). They are guilty of the sin of silence.

3. Withdraw. While some may pull away with a self-righteous desire to avoid contamination, this group may include many whose hearts are breaking. They may actually feel that to stay involved in the church puts their family's spiritual experience at risk. They may seek for fellowship in another church or a home church, often only to have their disappointment and disillusionment repeated.

4. Offer a proper protest. I believe this is God's plan for all who are genuinely concerned about the spirituality of the church. We protest because we want the church to be the best possible witness to the truths we are taking to the world. We protest because we love the souls of our fellow church members, and we want them to be corrected and saved at last. We protest because "indifference or neutrality in a religious crisis is regarded of God as a grievous crime; and equal to the very worst type of hostility against God" ("The Laodicean Church," *Review and Herald*, September 30, 1873). We protest because if obvious wrongs are ignored, "the blessing of the Lord is withheld from His people, and the innocent suffer with the guilty" ("The Cities of Refuge," *Signs of the Times*, January 20, 1881).

How to Protest the Wrongs in the Church

A small group of friends was visiting in our home one evening, and the discussion turned to our beloved church and some of its troublesome issues. Someone rather jokingly posed this question to the group, "How bad would things have to get before you would consider leaving the church?"

Tongue in cheek, one fellow said, "When they hire a woman preacher at my church, I'm down the road."

Again in a lighthearted mood, another said, "The day they move a rock band on stage, I won't be back."

And still another said, "The day the pastor introduces speaking in tongues, I'm out the door."

Each person named something that would supposedly make church attendance intolerable. I was surprised one of the ladies didn't try to even things out a bit by saying, "Yes, and when they appoint a man to lead women's ministries, I'm staying home."

We enjoyed our little act, but the serious question all of us should be asking is not what it would take for us to leave the church, but how bad things will have to get before we start protesting? And having answered that, the next question is how should we do that most effectively? Here are some suggestions:

1. Try to be realistic in your expectations of your fellow church members. It is only natural that people joining the Seventh-day Adventist church would expect a perfect message to produce perfect people. And when they find it otherwise, they become disheartened, complaining that the evils they had hoped to escape from in the world are in the church as well. "But we need not be thus disappointed," Ellen White writes, "for the Lord has not warranted us in coming to the conclusion that the church is perfect; and all our zeal will not be successful in making the church militant as pure as the church triumphant" (*Testimonies to Ministers and Gospel Workers*, p. 47).

"Militant" describes the church at war. During its engagement with the world and the devil, there are casualties, there are deserters, and there are even spies and saboteurs within its ranks.

But the militant church has another element that is critical to this discussion—it has everything from raw recruits to seasoned generals. A growing church will have members at different spiritual levels, from the mature to those just entering the pathway to the kingdom. That should be the kind of church all of us would want to belong to, but it requires us to be flexible and patient with our comrades in arms.

2. If you decide to address wrongs in the church, make sure you hold the right people accountable. "Make your complaint, plainly and openly, in the right spirit, to the proper ones" (*Testimonies for the Church*, vol. 9, p. 249). We must keep the lines of accountability clear if we are to make an intelligent protest. Individual members, local churches, conferences, and the General Conference all have different jurisdictions and different levels of accountability.

I occasionally meet Adventists who seem to think the local conference president has the authority and power to fix everything. He can certainly work to change conference programs and policies that are out of line, but he can do very little to change the behavior of individual church members. In reality, discipline of anyone who is a member of the Seventh-day Adventist church is done by the local church.[1] If things need fixing in your congregation or mine, we must count ourselves among the fixers.

Of course employees of the church may be reprimanded, transferred, or terminated by their employers, but such actions are not, strictly speaking, church discipline. Those people, too, all hold church membership somewhere, and if they are to be censured or dropped from membership, that will have to be done by their own local church.

We need to follow Matthew 18, where Jesus tells us to go to our brother with a spirit of reconciliation. "All things are of God, who has reconciled us to Himself through Jesus Christ, and has given us the ministry of reconciliation" (2 Corinthians 5:18). Listen carefully to the other person's point of view. Go with the attitude of a learner, rather than an instructor. Go to discover God's will, not to impose your own.

We are to approach others in humility with a keen sense of our own shortcomings. Have you noticed that sometimes those who were the most worldly, who claim to have committed every sin in the book when they were walking apart from Christ, are often the least tolerant of others' shortcomings? They are the kind that, even though they were in the church twenty years before they quit using caffeine, they expect everyone else to quit the same day they do. We must avoid falling into that category.

We must do our homework, check our sources, and even then be slow to assume we have all the facts. And, above all, let's not take for granted that what we have read on the Internet or in some scandal sheet is true.

3. Focus primarily on the spiritual health of the local church where you have membership. What good does it do to spend your life's energies trying to correct perceived problems in the local conference office, an Adventist university, or some medical center when your own church is floundering spiritually? You may have met people, as I have, who fret because they think the General Conference is getting too cozy with the World Council of Churches, but whose own church is failing to deal with a member's coziness with someone else's spouse. We need to address both.

We can, and we should, write letters and make telephone calls to church leaders at every level, but our influence outside our own congregation is limited. "If matters need adjusting at the head of the work, God will attend to that, and work to right every wrong" (*Selected Messages*, bk.2, p. 390). If things need to be put right in our own local congregation, let's work to correct those.

The very best protest we can make is to support church discipline in our own church. Regardless of how far adrift we may perceive the church at large to be, it is our privilege to stand in our local congregation and say, "It stops here!" We need to exercise responsibility where we have primary responsibility.

4. Strive for consistency and balance in your own life. It would be wonderful if all of us could say with Paul, "Imitate me, just as I also imitate Christ" (1 Corinthians 11:1). But we all have blind spots and stumble along. We all fall short. And while our right to protest is not contingent on our own perfection, we must be seen as persons who are putting forth sincere efforts to walk closely with Christ if we want to be taken seriously when we speak out against the wrongs of others. That only makes sense, doesn't it? You would not normally seek financial advice from one who is hopelessly in debt. Nor would you likely take counsel on how to repair your car from one who is walking because he tried to fix his.

Likewise, it doesn't make sense to complain because the church misspends money when we don't know how to manage our own. Or to be appalled at reports of Adventist young people using alcohol when we are killing ourselves from overeating and lack of exercise. Or to be known as an expert on the evils of TV when others wish we would give some study to the evils of harsh criticism.

Our own lives are the best possible protest against the wrongs we would like to see corrected in the church. "Individually we are to give, in the church where we are, an example of faithfulness and consecration" (*The Upward Look*, p. 274). The apostle says, "You are our epistle written in our hearts, known and read by all men" (2 Corinthians 3:2). We may never *write* a letter to the *Adventist Review*, but we can never escape *being* a letter.

5. Cultivate a positive outlook. The quickest way to be written off as a crank is to gain the reputation as one who knows nothing good about the church (or about much of anything). We should never permit ourselves to be found in that camp. Let those who hear our protests also hear us praising God for the advance of the work around the world. If things are not going well in our local church, let's thank God it isn't that way everywhere.

Here are some suggestions for putting a positive spin on our objections to things we feel are amiss:

How to Protest the Wrongs in the Church

- *Acknowledge the good.* For instance, if we share our concerns with our pastor or conference president, the first words out of our mouths should express appreciation for the heavy loads they carry. When we write a letter about an *Adventist Review* article that we think should never have been published, we should thank the editor for the many good articles.

- *Make your objection plainly but kindly.* Come directly to the point. Use the Bible and the Spirit of Prophecy to defend your position, but do not preach a sermon or present a large collection of Ellen White quotations.

- *Offer something better.* Whiners and complainers are not typically known for their creativity. They know "what's broke," but they don't know how to fix it. Looking on from the outside, everything looks so easy. Constructive criticism, by definition, is saying, "Here is a better way."

- *If possible and appropriate, offer to help.* It would be unusual if your pastor, the junior leader, the church school principal, and most other church leaders could not use some practical help that would elevate the spiritual level of your church.

Above all, let's not allow the shortcomings of others cause us to develop a "root of bitterness" and thereby lose our crown. We cannot let vengefulness and a get-even spirit corrupt our own souls. Ellen White uses the payment of tithe to illustrate this point, but other negative responses could serve just as well. "Some have been dissatisfied and have said: 'I will no longer pay my tithe; for I have no confidence in the way things are managed at the heart of the work.' But will you rob God because you think the management of the work is not right? . . . Send in your petitions for things to be adjusted and set in order; but do not withdraw from the work of God, and prove unfaithful, because others are not doing right" (*Testimonies for the Church*, vol. 9, p. 249).

6. Speak to the church from within the church. If we want to be taken seriously, we must participate fully in the life of the church. We must attend church business meetings, accept church offices, support the soul-winning efforts of the church, and be generous in our financial support. In other words, if we want to be a power for reform in the church, we must be "registered voters and taxpayers." If disgust or discouragement leads us to withdraw, we should not complain if the church goes ever deeper into apostasy. We have abdicated our right to be heard. If we take up residence outside the church, we will find that few people care what we think. They assume that once a person has gotten a divorce, he or she has no right to try to control his or her former spouse.

The core group is the measure of any church's spirituality. Instead of moving toward the fringe, move toward the center. Be where your voice, your vote, your influence counts most. Search for those who are like-minded and form a prayer circle, pleading with God to use you to help lift the standard higher.

7. Insist on due process. Typically, there will be committees and boards that have jurisdiction over certain aspects of church life—finance committee, music committee, social committee, board of elders, church board. Various questions that impact the spirituality of the church need to be resolved at those levels if at all possible. But if the issue is ignored or brushed aside, or if the offered solution does not harmonize with the plain teaching of God's Word, it may need to be candidly and courteously discussed in a business meeting. If a liberalizing element wants to make changes that are not in harmony with God's will, they should at least have to face their fellow church members in an open forum.

Every member has the right to insist on due process. That requires getting acquainted with the *Church Manual* and using it wisely and politely. The guidelines found in the *Church Manual* are there to protect the church from heavy-handed individuals who might want to bypass the

How to Protest the Wrongs in the Church

authority of the church and impose their wishes in areas not in harmony with Adventist principles.

8. Address issues early! Those who feel it their mission to unite the church with the world are often experts in lobbying, infiltration, and "creeping compromise." They are skillful and patient when it comes to taking very small steps in achieving their goals. Through prayer and the aid of the Holy Spirit, we should make ourselves competent in detecting early departures from God's will and intervening in a Christ-like spirit.

Joe Crews underscores that point emphatically in his book *Creeping Compromise*. "Conscientious church members delay getting involved and speaking out. They say they are waiting for a larger issue to present itself, then they will make their protest. But the devil will see to it that there never will be a larger issue" (p. 23).

9. Be courageous. Let's not allow ourselves to be drawn into a conspiracy of silence. Let's not sign on to a pact of mutual corruption that says, "If you don't mention my sins, I won't mention yours." God does not require us to listen without protest to the perversion of truth. He does not ask us to patiently stand by while our fellow members lead the church in following the customs and practices of the world. Moral judgments—thoughtful and careful, but explicit and unapologetic—need to be made.

Following is a familiar note of encouragement from Ellen White: "To stand in defense of truth and righteousness when the majority forsake us, to fight the battles of the Lord when champions are few—this will be our test. At this time we must gather warmth from the coldness of others, courage from their cowardice, and loyalty from their treason" (*Testimonies for the Church*, vol. 5, p. 136).

The pressure to conform is going to get worse. Perhaps the darkest side of all that Jesus foretold is found in the following words: "Now brother will betray brother to death, and the father his child; and children will rise up against parents and cause them to be put to death. And you will be hated by all for My name's sake. But he who endures to the end shall be saved" (Mark 13:12, 13). If we cannot endure the slights and rebuffs of fellow Adventists today, how will we endure *that* kind of treatment in some tomorrow?

Albert Einstein is credited with saying that if two percent of the population of the world refused any longer to sanction war, it could never happen again. That may be an overstatement, but the truth remains: A surprisingly small number of protestors can make an amazing difference. The reason is simple: Our society has been taught to be non-judgmental. They have been reared on a heavy diet of self-esteem. They are well schooled in political correctness. So when *even one person* has the courage to call sin by its right name, it sends shock waves through the ranks of the compromisers and the complacent.

Being courageous doesn't mean being belligerent or obnoxious, nor does it mean being so "loving" that our lips are sealed. It is the right blend of humility, kindness, and firmness.

10. Pray for the church. And while we pray, let's not forget that *we* are the church. Guard against cultivating an "us-and-them" mindset. Study the beautiful prayers of Daniel and Ezra. Notice how these godly men accept ownership of the church's faults. "O Lord, . . . we have sinned and committed iniquity, we have done wickedly and rebelled" (Daniel 9:4, 5). "O my God, I am too ashamed and humiliated to lift up my face to You, my God; for our iniquities have risen higher than our heads, and our guilt has grown up to the heavens" (Ezra 9:6). These are the best models I know of "sighing and crying" for the sins of the church. Also, as we pray, let's remember that the church belongs to Jesus. He is far more burdened for its moral uprightness than any of us are.

11. Trust in God and the prophetic future of the church. I have more to say on this later, but a careful study of the subject will show that the church will be purified, not disowned; pruned, not uprooted; sifted and shaken, but not thrown away or spit out.

So be patient, my friend! Our best efforts to keep the church on course will not succeed in bringing reformation to the lives of everyone. But our Christ-like example and gentle objections will strengthen and encourage the conscientious, increasing the number who will remain in the garner when the chaff is blown away.

So how can we be courageous protestors and work for unity at the same time? We'll address that challenging question next.

Discussion Questions:
1. Which of the four responses to perceived wrongs in the church are you most likely to take? Which response is most characteristic of the members of your congregation?
2. Do you feel the leaders in your local church are conscientiously trying to keep up with church discipline as problems arise?
3. Do you know with some certainty what conduct by church members is subject to church discipline?
4. How can you maintain a positive outlook when you have certain knowledge about widespread apostasy in the church?
5. Are there members in your congregation who seem to be an expert at offering "something better"? Have you seen that work to keep potential problems from developing?

Endnotes

1   *Seventh-day Adventist Church Manual* (Hagerstown: Review and Herald Publishing Association, 2000), 175-190.

Chapter Eight

WHAT A UNITED CHURCH LOOKS LIKE

> *"I do not pray for these alone, but also for those who will believe in Me through their word; that they all may be one as You, Father, are in Me, and I in you; that they also may be one in Us, that the world may believe that You sent Me"* (John 17:20, 21).

The shadow of the cross falls across the kneeling form of the Savior. The great divine Shepherd is soon to be separated from His tiny flock, and He prays for them with intense feeling. The consummate miracle worker of the universe is Himself asking His Father to work a miracle that far surpasses the raising of the dead. *He prays for the unity of the church.* "That they may be one," He implores, "just as We are one" (John 17:22).

That prayer has often made me pause and shake my head in wonder. Is Jesus really asking that His followers be united as closely as the members of the Godhead—that mysterious tri-unity that baffles the keenest minds? Is that kind of unity even remotely possible for sinful human beings? What would a church so united look like? What would have to happen in your congregation and mine for that prayer to be answered?

The devil must smile at the very suggestion. He has successfully divided human beings in countless ways—along racial lines, national identity, level of education, political preference, economic status—not to mention the built-in divisiveness of our perverse and self-serving carnal natures. And it only seems to get worse when you enter the realm of religion. Historians have said that the majority of all wars have been religious wars. (What an oxymoron that is!) But you don't have to read history books to realize that; all you have to do is watch the evening news.

What a United Church Looks Like

There you are apt to see religious conflict somewhere in our world—Protestants and Catholics killing each other, Jews and Muslims blowing each other to bits, Buddhists and Hindus torching each others' temples.

The hundreds of factions in the Christian church have made religion the object of scorn for many. How are non-Christians supposed to be attracted to a people who hold up their Bible as the great moral guide for mankind when so few of them can agree on what it says? Why would the secular man seek fellowship in a group that preaches the gospel of love when that love is so apparently lacking in their own families and congregations?

The challenge to imitate the oneness of the Godhead forces us to closely examine our definition of unity. This is not a grin-and-bear-it exercise. It goes beyond just forgetting our differences and trying to find common ground. The secular person can do that. People in politics and business do that routinely. Husbands and wives may stay together for the sake of the kids. Common causes unite. A oneness like that of the Trinity, however, is light years beyond such fragile human accords. It falls far outside anything that can be achieved by skillful diplomacy or brilliant management. It is a spiritual unity, a oneness achieved by loving as God loves.

Jesus' reason for His request to the Father is "that the world may know that You have sent Me" (John 17:23). "That the world may know." No wonder the world will notice! If a united church were to appear on the horizon, the world would be sure to take notice. It would be as the rose of peace among the thorns, the dove of peace among the vultures, the sweet song of peace among the dissonance and rancor of competing factions. A unified church advertises that it is led by a supernatural Leader, that it is has been infused with a supernatural power, that it is not just another human institution. People in our deeply divided world, if not drawn to join such a group, would at least view it with admiration.

Is the Seventh-day Adventist church that church? Surely, when you get to the door of the remnant, the quarreling stops! Of course that assessment will have to be made on a congregation-by-congregation basis, but severe internal strife is not unknown among God's people. The prophet to the remnant writes, "Nothing short of the miraculous power of God can bring human beings with their different temperaments together in harmonious action" (*Testimonies for the Church*, vol. 9, p. 194). And that includes the "human beings" within the remnant.

Still, Jesus prays for that miracle. Is He asking for something impossible for us to achieve? No. The Father is waiting and anxious to answer His Son's prayer.

So what does a united church look like?

As if to answer our question, the apostle Paul gives us the formula for unity in Ephesians 4:3-6 where he first invites us to endeavor "to keep the unity of the Spirit in the bond of peace," and then clearly defines what those bonds are in his list of seven "ones." "There is one body and one Spirit, just as you were called in one hope of your calling; one Lord, one faith, one baptism; one God and Father of all, who is above all, and through all, and in you all."

First, there is one body. Paul expands the body metaphor for the church in 1 Corinthians 12:14 where he says, "For in fact the body in not one member but many." The physical body consists of fingers, arms, legs, ears, eyes, and so on. None of these were created independently and then assembled. They all developed from a common beginning, a single cell. The body's parts have never had an independent existence. There is an inherent and essential unity in the body. Separation from the body means death.

The same is true of the church. Unity begins with belonging. Not just names-on-the-books belonging, but believing and acting as if belonging is crucial. Those in a united church do not doubt that they belong to one body, the remnant of Bible prophecy. They know that they live and function and survive only in connection with the body.

What a United Church Looks Like

Christ and His cause are central in the lives of those who are truly united. They do not see themselves as solitary pilgrims, fighting alone against fierce opponents, making their way toward the celestial city; they belong to a body of believers who travel the upward path beside them. These are not just casual acquaintances; they are bound together by the most powerful bonds human beings can know. Self-interest is replaced by a consuming passion for the welfare of their fellow travelers.

During the Korean War, the North Koreans captured prisoners from all of the allied forces, held them in terrible conditions, and treated them inhumanely. When the war was over, some researchers decided to compare survival rates of the different national groups. They discovered that survival depended primarily on just one attitude. Among some groups the mindset that prevailed—expressed or not—was: "If anyone makes it, *I* will make it." That put them in competition with each other for every scrap of food, for any extra blankets and clothing, and for the warmest spot in the shelter. Their survival rate was the worst.

Among one group the outlook that prevailed was this: "If anyone makes it, we will *all* make it." They shared everything. They particularly shared their meager rations with those who were ill. And their survival rate was by far the best.

The attitude of the latter group will prevail in a united church. "If anyone in our group makes it to the kingdom, we are all going to make it. I will risk my life to see that that happens." That was Moses' response when God threatened to wipe out the whole nation of Israel. "Take my life, too," he volunteered. "I'm one of them." (See Exodus 32:31, 32). Can you imagine belonging to a church that looks like *that*?

Secondly, there is one Spirit. Ephesians 4:3 says, "endeavoring to keep the unity of the Spirit in the bond of peace." The Holy Spirit is the Spirit of unity. He is a Person; He cannot be divided. He cannot be made to grant to one what He denies to another. He teaches the same truths to all and convicts all by the same moral standard. He is the mysterious, powerful agency that melts away differences and makes people love each other and work together. He helps us to "stand fast in one spirit, with one mind striving together for the faith of the gospel" (Philippians 1:27). The Spirit works, first of all, to dispel the divisions that exist in our own lives, those inner disharmonies that make our own souls a constant battlefield. A person not at peace with God and himself will not, and cannot, be at peace with others.

One of the unsolved mysteries of ornithology is the ability of large flocks of small birds to wheel, climb, and bank simultaneously and at high speed. There is no apparent leader as in a neat line of geese. So who decides to turn sharply to the right while descending? And even more baffling, how is that "decision" communicated in a microsecond to the other thousand-plus birds in the flock? They seem to be powerfully bonded to each other by an invisible "spirit," to be of "one mind," to the point of even being able to *anticipate* the next maneuver![1]

We know the Spirit is at work when a spirit of love and caring pervades our congregation. I was working on a display for a conference constituency meeting and could not get a certain mechanical feature to work. It was nearing nine o'clock at night, and I was getting desperate. I had to have the thing set up and working at the meeting site, which was seventy miles away, by eight o'clock the next morning. I called my mechanically-gifted friend Al and started to explain. He interrupted me saying, "You don't have to explain, Lee Roy; if it matters to you, it matters to me. I'll be right over."

I felt both honored and embarrassed that anyone would make such an unqualified commitment to my needs. But I believe that kind of commitment will be common in a united church. "If it matters to you, it matters to me" is a theme that will guide its relationships. "Those who are united to Christ by the truth of heavenly origin should have strong friendship for one another. . . . In Christ Jesus there is love, and those who are united

What a United Church Looks Like

to Christ will not have merely a tame, common regard as acquaintances, but true, sincere love for one another" (*The Ellen G. White 1888 Materials*, p. 1141).

Our church families need to be more like the early church where it is said they "had all things in common, and sold their possessions and goods, and divided them among all, as anyone had need" (Acts 2:44, 45). If that defined our church relationships today, what a powerful difference that would make! Our lifestyle would not be determined by our individual family's resources—what *we* can afford—it would be determined by our *church family's* needs. If there are young people in my church who cannot afford to pay the tuition to go to church school or academy, it might mean I cannot "afford" to go to Hawaii for vacation, or that I need to drive my car another year.

Third, there is one hope. We all have our own set of hopes that give direction to our lives each day. Some young people hope to finish college and enter a chosen profession. Those who have achieved that goal are hoping to find a worthy companion and enjoy family life. Middle-aged people hope for a stable economy so they can keep their jobs. Older people hope to escape serious illness and stay out of a nursing home.

But there is only one hope. It is not found in salvaging a failing economy or in stopping global warming, as much as we would like to see those problems remedied. The one hope, the only hope for our world is the return of Jesus. In Titus 2:13 it is called the "blessed hope." It is a powerful bond in the Adventist circle. When you walk into an Adventist church, the very atmosphere should be charged with hope. Perhaps no one thinks of the Second Coming in the same way Seventh-day Adventists do. It thrills us. It unites us. It makes heaven seem very near. And it should be a constant and powerful reminder that if we are going to live together without spoiling the harmony of heaven, we must learn to get along here.

Fourth, Paul points out that we have one Lord. In discussions about the kind of person Jesus is, I have heard the comment, "Well, that's not the Jesus *I* know," making it sound as if one has a choice among several. But there is only one Lord. There has never been anyone like Him. He stands alone in the absolute glory of His uniqueness. He is the "brightness of His [Father's] glory and the express image of His person" (Hebrews 1:3). He is the God of the Old Testament, the New Testament, and the twenty-first century.

"Lord" denotes someone who is in charge, someone who has authority. That is Jesus, the Head of the church (Ephesians 5:23). He, like the Spirit, is a divine Person and cannot be divided. He is the Head of the one body. He cannot be made to serve as the Head of hundreds of opposing denominations and factions. He cannot be made the Head of even one Adventist congregation whose members are quarreling. Those who surrender to His authority are united. And that means they will experience a uniform separation from the world.

Ellen White asks the question: "Then as the children of God are one in Christ, how does Jesus look upon caste, upon society distinctions, upon the division of man from his fellow man, because of color, race, position, wealth, birth, or attainments? The secret of unity is found in the equality of believers in Christ. The reason for all division, discord, and difference is found in separation from Christ" (*Selected Messages*, bk. 1, p. 259).

The divisions Ellen White mentions in the foregoing statement—race, position, wealth, etc.—are only illustrations of the real divider. That is called *self*. We can call it self-esteem, self-importance, self-righteousness, self-serving, self-promotion—it doesn't matter. The root is a self separated from Christ, and the fruit is division in the church.

When Paul heard of some divisions in the church in Corinth, he said, "I am told that one is saying 'I am of Paul,' and another says, 'I am of Apollos,' and another says, 'I am of Cephas.'" He then asks a probing question: "Is Christ divided?" (See 1 Corinthians 1:10-17). "He in whose heart Christ abides recognizes Christ abiding in the heart of his brother. Christ never wars against Christ.

What a United Church Looks Like

Christ never exerts an influence against Christ. Christians are to do their work, whatever it may be, in the unity of the Spirit for the perfecting of the whole body" (*My Life Today*, p. 276).

Number five on Paul's list is the idea of one faith. The idea that there are multiple ways to heaven is shot down. Paul warns the Galatians: "If we, or an angel from heaven, preach any other gospel to you than what we have preached to you, let him be accursed" (Galatians 1:8). Pretty strong! There is a faith that is fixed. There is a truth that is settled. Our lack of study, our prejudiced study, even our most sincere study, if it reaches conclusions that cannot be endorsed by the one body and the one Spirit and the one Lord, it does not qualify as the one faith! The members of a united church may have minor theological differences, but they are solidly united on the platform of truth.

"The present truth is not difficult to be understood, and the people whom God is leading will be united upon this broad, firm platform. He will not use individuals of different faith, opinions, and views, to scatter and divide. Heaven and holy angels are working to unite, to bring into the unity of the faith, into the one body" (*Testimonies for the Church*, vol. 1, p. 327).

Unity is the natural, inevitable consequence of what the truth does in us. Paul does not ask us to work hard at *creating* unity but to "keep the unity of the Spirit in the bond of peace" (Ephesians 4:3). We are challenged to protect what the truth has already created. We do that by constantly aligning ourselves with revealed truth, not by compromising principle in order to gear in with those opposed to truth.

Jesus made it clear that His teachings would bring division. "For I have come to 'set a man against his father, a daughter against her mother, and a daughter-in-law against her mother-in-law'; and 'a man's enemies will be those of his own household'" (Matthew 10:35, 36). Jesus did not expect there to be perfect unity between wheat and tares, sheep and goats. He knew that the unity

He prayed for would ultimately be achieved through the separation of those diverse elements.

We, too, need to recognize that God sometimes divides, and Satan sometimes unites; that unity is not always good and division always bad; and that peaceful coexistence and the absence of conflict are not the same as unity. There are some things that should never be united and some things that should never be divided.[2]

"It is a grave mistake on the part of those who are children of God to seek to bridge the gulf that separates the children of light from the children of darkness by yielding principle, by compromising the truth" ("Principle Never to Be Sacrificed," *Review and Herald,* July 24, 1894).

Then there is one baptism. Baptism by immersion in water is the only baptism the Bible teaches and heaven accepts. It alone symbolizes death to sin, a resurrection to a new life of obedience, a cleansing of guilt, and a separation from the world. It publicly declares one's union with the body of Christ. We are baptized in the name of the one Father, and the one Son, and the one Holy Spirit into the one faith.

Unity regarding a correct doctrine of baptism is to be commended, but something more is needed. Members in a united church will hold each other accountable to their baptismal vows. A united church will be well-disciplined.

Finally, there is one God and Father. What a beautiful climax to this picture of unity! We belong to the family of God. We have the same Father. We are no longer strangers, aliens, or outcasts. We have a sheltering home in the family of God, His church. Having one Father is a powerfully uniting factor.

The foregoing elements that define unity cannot be divided. I cannot say, "I may not have my doctrine straight, but I know in my heart that I have the Holy Spirit." Or, "I may not belong to the right body, but I have the one Lord, Jesus Christ." Or, "I may not have been baptized according to the Bible mode, but I have the one faith, and that's what counts." That will not work. Such talk describes division, not the level of unity Jesus prayed for.

Spurious theories of unity

We are at war, and it is tempting to sacrifice almost anything to keep the troops united. Out of desperation we have begun redefining ourselves—our identity and our mission—in order to curb desertions. The ultimate capitulation is the redefining of unity itself. That has led to the invention and promotion of counterfeit theories of unity in the church today that should never have been given a hearing. Even though I have separated them under different labels, in reality there is a great deal of similarity and overlap.

Unity in diversity - Rightly understood, this concept can be a great blessing to the church. Unity in diversity is just what Paul preached. His gospel testifies to God's power to take people of differing religions, genders, and economic backgrounds and produce "one new man" (Ephesians 2:15). The dividing partitions are gone. In this "one new man" there would still be a diversity of gifts and personality, but there is no evidence Paul intended for ethnic and cultural differences to trump a Bible-based doctrine and lifestyle. All would still be strongly united and identified by the seven "ones."

Today, "unity in diversity" has become a mantra of the liberalizing element in the church. Its proponents give strong advocacy to the premise that the church must open its doors ever wider in order to welcome and accommodate people of all cultures and lifestyles, even those cultures and lifestyles that may not align with Adventist beliefs. Culture, they say, is a wonderfully enriching element.

But if culture is "right," then what about the American culture? Is not its culture of fast food, TV, sports, nudity, alcohol, and rock music also "right"? That is the not-so-subtle implication of the argument. There is no biblical support for a cultural accommodation that sets aside those lifestyle practices that define the Christian.

Theological pluralism - Theological pluralism is the acceptance of different doctrinal positions *within* a denomination. Historically, those who had a serious doctrinal difference with their church would leave and establish a new denomination. But today, in order to keep as many members as possible under one denominational roof, "pluralism" has been invented. It is the natural fallout from the unity-in-diversity argument. Eventually, if one is going to defend the incorporation of unacceptable lifestyle practices, there needs to be some adjustment in how the doctrinal positions of the church that address those issues are perceived. Something must be done to alleviate the nagging guilt of being in violation of one's baptismal vows. Theological pluralism serves that function by developing a rationale for including divergent views—not a sound rationale, but one that simply ignores what the Bible and the Spirit of Prophecy teaches on those subjects.

In practice, theological pluralism is often demonstrated by the creation of more than one Sabbath worship service in many of our churches. That is defensible, of course, if there are more people than can be seated in one service. But in many, if not most cases, the real reason is to redefine the church in order to keep everyone happy and attending. It is a strategy of compromise and accommodation. Churches that resort to that remedy openly advertise that they are deeply divided.

Theological pluralism deprives us of the ability or willingness to differentiate between truth and heresy. For fear of offending some, sermons are preached that offend none. If everyone's right, no one is wrong. We must all study to know the difference between the pillars of our faith and those things that the Bible and Spirit of Prophecy do not speak with finality, or subjects on which the Holy Spirit has not yet brought the church to a consensus. That will help us know where to be firm and where to be flexible.

Core beliefs - While pluralism seeks unity through an open acceptance of differing beliefs, "core beliefs" seeks

What a United Church Looks Like

unity through making requirements for membership as small as possible. It is argued that our Adventist identity takes in way too much territory; twenty-eight fundamental beliefs are just too much to keep in mind, much less to practice. Therefore, we should consider dramatically reducing qualifications for membership. This is accomplished by requiring "unity on the essentials" while allowing "diversity on the non-essentials."

This poses two challenging questions. First, what are the essentials, and what are the non-essentials? The Adventist evangelicals among us are working hard to shrink the list down to their version of the gospel. For them, the doctrines of the sanctuary, the Spirit of Prophecy, the remnant, and the three angels' messages are non-essentials. That goes also for anything that has to do with lifestyle—diet, dress, music, Sabbath-keeping, entertainment, etc.

Second question: Who decides? That's easy. The local congregation decides; not by vote usually, but by default; that is, by whatever the common practice is. Open discussion and debate are avoided at all costs. In practice, this is congregationalism, the ultimate form of disunity. We need to ask ourselves this: Have we come to the place where we are willing to say that *anything* God asks is *non-essential?*

Readers of the *Adventist Review* were told several years ago to expect change—that the uniformity in belief and practice we presently enjoy will eventually be overwhelmed by our burgeoning membership. "Eventually Adventism will have to decide either to allow cultural variations or to forbid them with all the risks of schism involved in such a course. It is probable that the denomination will have to decide between those things that are essential for Adventism and those items or practices that might vary from one culture to the next."[3] In my view, to follow where that kind of thinking leads is to make schism certain and the Adventist church of the future unrecognizable.

The gospel of tolerance - This is not actually a separate strategy for unity but an umbrella under which all of the foregoing take shelter. In practice, tolerance seeks unity through *silence*. Its advocates believe that the absence of dissent is the best possible definition of unity. They tell us that if we will just be quiet about lifestyle issues, stop giving correction and reproof, and talk of nothing but Jesus and His love, we will achieve the unity Christ prayed for.

According to this "gospel," *intolerance* is the church's gravest sin. In fact, it is virtually the only serious sin left. It is the one sin even the most gentle pastors do not hesitate to condemn. Intolerant people must be shamed and silenced. They are rightfully vilified as judgmental and legalistic. "Hate the sin, love the sinner" is no longer allowed. Sin and sinners are too closely linked to permit that kind of objective separation.

We need to remind ourselves that when we joined the fellowship of light, we chose of our own free will to walk in the light. And within that fellowship we are to maintain unity through holding each other accountable, not through being silent.

The power of unity

So we ask again, did Jesus pray for the impossible? If not, how can we help answer His prayer? I would add two additional things. First, we need to look at the great blessings that come to a united church. "In unity there is a life, a power, that can be obtained in no other way. There will be a vast power in the church when the energies of the members are united under the control of the Spirit. Then will God be able to work mightily through His people for the conversion of sinners" (*Testimonies for the Church*, vol. 7, p. 236). If the prospect of being energized by that "vast power" does not excite us and unite us, what will?

Secondly, we need to candidly assess the cost of disunity. We must see how it weakens us spiritually, how it derails our mission, how it absorbs time and energy that should be invested in warning and winning the lost, and how it leaves behind a multitude of the hurting and disenchanted.

What a United Church Looks Like

Jesus prayed for a level of unity that is indeed mind-boggling—"that they all may be one, as You, Father, are in Me, and I in You" (John 17:21). We are to be one in *nature* as They are because we have all become "partakers of the divine nature" (2 Peter 1:4). We are to be one in *character* as They are because we all imitate the same Model (1 Peter 2:21). We are to be one in *purpose* as They are because we all are engaged with Them in taking the gospel to all the world in this generation (Matthew 28:19,20).

Next, we want to discuss further how to relate to those who, whether in sincerity or with malice, are causing division in the church.

Discussion Questions:

1. Review the "seven ones" that are to unite the church. Is there anything missing? Would the church be perfectly united if these were incorporated into personal, family, and church life?
2. Do you agree that there are some things that should divide us? If so, what?
3. How do you understand the "unity in diversity" concept and how it should be applied to church life?
4. What can you do as an individual to foster greater unity in your church without compromising principle?
5. Ask yourself, "Do I work to unite or divide?" How ready am I to break the unity of the church?

Endnotes

1. The Straight Dope, "How does a flock of birds wheel and swoop in unison?" http://www.straightdope.com/columns/read/2151/how-does-a-flock-of-birds-wheel-and-swoop-in-unison (accessed December 29, 2008).
2. Paraphrased from Samuel Koranteng-Pipim, "True and Counterfeit Unity," *Here We Stand* (Hagerstown: Review and Herald Graphics, 2005), 754-756.
3. "The Church and Change," *The Adventist Review*, Millennial Issue (January 2000).

Chapter Nine

SOME WOLVES WEAR WOOL SUITS

"Beware of false prophets, who come to you in sheep's clothing, but inwardly they are ravenous wolves" (Matthew 7:15).

Many a wolf, as he lies in wait or circles the flock in search of the opportune moment, may secretly wish he could slip into a sheepskin and boldly approach his unsuspecting prey. Jesus warned His followers of just such a danger—vicious predators, "ravenous wolves," disguised as their innocent victims, poised to make a raid on the flock. Peter, also, gives a clear warning: "There will be false teachers among you, who will secretly bring in destructive heresies . . . And many will follow their destructive ways, because of whom the way of truth will be blasphemed" (2 Peter 2:1, 2). John joins in, saying, "Beloved, do not believe every spirit, but test the spirits, whether they are of God; because many false prophets have gone out into the world" (1 John 4:1).

With so many red flags waving, one would think the saints would be more guarded, less likely to be taken in. But it seems all it takes for some people to be deceived is for the wolves to show up in perfectly-tailored, well-pressed wool suits. The saints are armed and ready to do battle with the beast and the dragon—not with charismatic laymen and credentialed ministers.

It would take volumes to discuss the various species of "wolves" that God's people should be prepared to recognize and defend themselves against, but in this chapter, it is my purpose to narrow the discussion to the agenda of just two: those that are variously labeled "dissidents," "off-shoots," "independents," "far right," etc.; and those on the liberalizing, compromising "left."

Individuals in the first group make up those who have little or no sympathy with, or loyalty to, the organized Seventh-day Adventist church. They tend to operate as a separate church, and in fact, many see themselves as constituting the "true remnant." Those in the second group work through the organizational structure of the church to set its direction away from biblical Adventism, seeking to make it more evangelical and conformable to the popular culture. Their agenda is typically accomplished by common consent, rather than by open discussion of issues.

However, make no mistake; it is the intent of both groups to change the church. If those on the right were to prevail, the church would fragment into thousands of independent Pharisaical cells. If those on the left continue to prevail (as they are currently), the church could eventually merge with evangelical Christianity.

I will present two sets of questions that might help in discerning the purposes and tactics of such individuals and groups. First, some questions to ask ourselves.

Am I well-grounded in the doctrinal positions of the Seventh-day Adventist church? There are none as vulnerable as the uninformed. They are "tossed to and fro and carried about with every wind of doctrine" (Ephesians 4:14). And "when the shaking comes, by the introduction of false theories, these surface readers, anchored nowhere, are like shifting sand" (*Testimonies to Ministers and Gospel Workers*, p. 112).

"Those who have accepted the truth of the third angel's message are to hold it fast by faith; and it will hold them from drifting into superstitions and theories that would separate them from one another and from God. Our reception of the truth we hold as Seventh-day Adventists was not a chance experience. It was reached by earnest prayer and careful research of the Inspired Word" ("As Ye Have Received . . . So Walk," *Review and Herald*, August 19, 1909).

I don't believe God's servant is encouraging anyone to accept without question what the pioneers painstakingly hammered out a hundred and fifty years ago. Rather, I hear her saying, "Test it; study it out thoroughly; but *settle it!*" It is dangerous to go along day after day in the fog of uncertainty.

Do I have a matured loyalty and commitment to the Seventh-day Adventist church as a divinely-ordained movement? Like any good predator, a wolf has a keen sense of sight and smell. He marks well those sheep that always feed at the fringe of the flock. He can, just by sniffing the wind, tell where each is with respect to the shepherd and the fold.

If you are prone to feed on the fringe, to hang back, to avoid getting right into the middle of things in the church, you can be sure you are being closely monitored by the devil and his agents. If you harbor doubts about the remnant status of the Seventh-day Adventist church—its message, its mission, its authority—there is no way you can honestly deny your susceptibility to deception. Your knowledge of doctrine, your hard-headed commitment to the truth, your bold assertion of loyalty to the Spirit of Prophecy—none of these will save you from deception. If your loyalty is weak, you have sold your best armor to the devil. You can be sure he already views you as his lawful prey.

Many years ago, I worked for a conference president who, in appealing to his staff to be thoroughly loyal to the Seventh-day Adventist church, went so far as to say we should have "a kind of belligerent loyalty." I cringed a bit at the term "belligerent" but tried to understand. It was not until I read the following from Clifford Goldstein, however, that I *really* understood. "By the grace of God, the only way I'd leave the Adventist church is if I was thrown out—and I would still send it my tithe! If the Adventist church sent my tithe money to Saddam Hussein, I'd continue to be a Seventh-day Adventist."[1]

Do I have a keen appetite for hearing about the shortcomings of the church's institutions and its leaders? If you subscribe to any of the several muckraking publications available, if your ears are open and eager to hear about the latest Adventist college campus scandal, the infidelity of some pastor, the misuse of funds by some conference committee, it is safe to predict that the day will come when you will find yourself *outside* of the Seventh-day Adventist church.

Sour grapes do not make sweet wine. The tragedy of focusing on the negative is that it leaves too little time and brain space to enjoy and participate in the really good things that are happening in the church.

Do I have an unusual curiosity about "new light," innovative interpretations of Bible prophecy, or "far-out" ideas about anything religious? Are you the kind of person who has a consuming interest in such things as the Old Testament year-of-jubilee cycle, the idea that every time prophecy in the Bible will be repeated in literal time in the last days, or that Israel really will be a major player in end-time events? Are you one who is easily caught up in Adventist "hot potatoes" issues? Are you the type who would spend thousands of dollars (if you had them) to go looking for Noah's ark or the Ark of the Covenant?

In addition, are you fascinated by claims that provide quick fixes for health problems but that ignore the principles of the Adventist health message? This topic may not seem to fit in with our discussion right here, but we live in the time of the Omega of apostasy, and we have reason to believe that that deception, like the Alpha, could combine religious deception and spiritualistic approaches to resolving health issues.

The bottom line? Beware of becoming an "Athenian Adventist"—one who lives "either to tell, or to hear some new thing" (Acts 17:21). Perhaps the best response to such invitations is that which Nehemiah gave to his detractors: "'I am doing a great work, so that I cannot come down'" (Nehemiah 6:3). If you and I are busy serving others, we'll have a lot less time to listen to the devil's line.

Am I either very satisfied or terribly dissatisfied with my own spiritual condition and/or the spiritual nurturing I receive through the church? Either of these extremes makes us susceptible. An individual who thinks he knows enough, prays enough, obeys enough surely fits the self-satisfied condition Jesus finds in Laodicea. The devil is anxious that the sleep of those who are "good enough" not be disturbed.

But while all of us need to hear the call to "come up higher," we need to recognize that a nagging burden of guilt and lack of peace also makes us susceptible. The devil's predators have no scruples against offering sympathy and spiritual renewal as a way of winning our confidence and luring us away from the fold. They will intimate that we are not being fed where we are and that they will give us better food. But be assured; their rations are full of poison.

How did you score? If you said "yes" to the first two questions and "no" to the last three, you should be fairly well prepared to identify wolves regardless of how they are dressed. Now I want you to reflect on some questions to ask of or about those who would entice you, your family, or friends to push against the fence or to leave the church's sheltering fold altogether.

Do they profess to have "new light," and does that "light" have a tendency to unsettle faith in the generally accepted doctrinal positions held by Seventh-day Adventists? "Men and women will arise professing to have some new light or some new revelation whose tendency is to unsettle faith in the old landmarks. Their doctrines will not bear the test of God's word, yet souls will be deceived" (*Testimonies for the Church*, vol. 5, p. 295). "We are in continual danger of getting above the simplicity of the gospel. There is an intense desire on the part of many to startle the world with something original, that shall lift the people into a state of spiritual ecstasy" (*Selected Messages*, bk. 2, p. 23).

New interpretations of Bible prophecy, new revelations regarding the nature of the deity, new understandings of righteousness by faith—these are the tested and tried traps for the unwary. Now, it is not wrong for any of us to come up with new understandings of what the

Bible teaches. In fact, that is encouraged. It's how the next question is answered that makes all the difference.

Are they willing to have their beliefs reviewed by "brethren of experience," and are they ready to accept their counsel? God has given us the "multitude-of-counselors" principle in Proverbs 11:14. The Seventh-day Adventist church has carefully-spelled-out policies for examining and accepting or rejecting so-called new light. Those who are unwilling to submit their views to that process should not be trusted. Observance of this one rule alone would keep thousands from being pulled into the whirlpool of deception.

"God has not passed His people by and chosen one solitary man here and another there as the only ones worthy to be entrusted with His truth. He does not give one man new light contrary to the established faith of the body. . . . The only safety for any of us is in receiving no new doctrine, no new interpretation of the Scriptures, without first submitting it to brethren of experience. Lay it before them in a humble, teachable spirit, with earnest prayer; and if they see no light in it, yield to their judgment" (*Testimonies for the Church*, vol. 5, pp. 291-293).

Why wouldn't anyone be willing to do that? First, it might be because they are afraid their ideas will not pass muster. Second, it could be because they believe they are especially taught and directed by God Himself. Why would they submit to other human beings when God is giving revelations directly to them?

"There have ever been individuals of independent minds who have claimed that they were right, that God had especially taught, impressed, and led them. Each has a theory of his own, views peculiar to himself, and each claims that his views are in accordance with the word of God" (*Testimonies for the Church*, vol. 3, p. 428).

Do they appear to be overly pious? I hesitate to put this on the list because it is so obviously subjective. On the other hand, it is right here that the sheep get the wool pulled over their eyes. It is the *apparent sincerity and piety* of the predators that is so disarming. And some of them are sincere! They really believe they are led of God to do what they are doing. And their expressions of confidence in the Lord's leading, their uninhibited freedom in praising the Lord—these open the hearts of those who sincerely want a deeper spiritual experience.

"Men professing to have new light, claiming to be reformers, will have great influence over a certain class who are convinced of the heresies that exist in the present age and who are not satisfied with the spiritual condition of the churches. With true, honest hearts, these desire to see a change for the better, a coming up to a higher standard. . . . Someone making high profession as a reformer comes to them, as Satan came to Christ disguised as an angel of light, and draws them still further from the path of right" (*Testimonies for the Church*, vol. 5, p.144).

Notice that Ellen White takes the analogy far beyond the attempt of a wolf to clothe itself in sheepskin; she says these pretenders come "disguised as an angel of light." Again, the reason so many of the saints are taken in by the sophistries of these charlatans is that they talk, look, and act so *spiritual*. Who would dare turn a deaf ear to "an angel of light?"

How tragic it is that those who are "dissatisfied with the spiritual condition of the churches" and who "desire to see a change for the better," allow themselves to be led down a path that leads them further into darkness! A safer course would be to stay in the church and by their lives and testimony seek to elevate its spiritual condition.

Do they avoid church leaders and seasoned members and prey upon new believers? If you see some stranger showing an unusual interest in the newly baptized members of your congregation, do not hesitate to alert the watchmen. "Also from among yourselves will men rise up, speaking perverse things, to draw away the disciples after themselves" (Acts 20:30). These wolves are much too wise to go head-to-head with seasoned members of the church. Nothing demonstrates their true character more than their attempts to subvert the minds of those immature in faith and experience.

Is theirs a negative message, finding fault with nearly everyone and everything in the church, while positive reports of the advance of the gospel are ignored? When David was encouraged by his men to pin Saul to the ground with his spear, he said, "The Lord forbid that I should do this thing to my master, the Lord's anointed, to stretch forth mine hand against him, seeing he is the anointed of the Lord" (1 Samuel 24:6). It is truly amazing that David would call the murderous Saul "the anointed of the Lord" and would not lift his hand against him. Yet how easily many today dare bring a "reviling accusation" (2 Peter 2:11) against God's appointed leaders, the great majority of whom are conscientious and hard working.

"There are many who find special enjoyment in discoursing and dwelling upon the defects, whether real or imaginary, of those who bear heavy responsibilities in connection with the institutions of God's cause. They overlook the good that has been accomplished, the benefits that have resulted from arduous labor and unflinching devotion to the cause" (*Testimonies for the Church*, vol. 4, p. 196). They overlook the good, but have nothing better to offer. I have wanted to ask such critics, "Where is *your* Mission Spotlight?"

"When anyone is drawing apart from the organized body of God's commandment-keeping people, when he begins to weigh the church in his human scales, and begins to pronounce judgment against them, then you may know that God is not leading him. He is on the wrong track" (*Selected Messages*, bk. 3, p. 18).

Do they seem to have connections across the country and around the world, and do they show sympathy with other "ministries" that are working against, or at least outside of, the organized church? "A line of unbelief stretches across the continent and is in communication with the church of God. Its influence has been exerted to undermine confidence in the work of the Spirit of God" (*Testimonies for the Church*, vol. 5, p. 294). It is not right to make someone guilty simply by association, but we need to be aware of connections that may help us make an accurate assessment of the person or "ministry" we are evaluating.

Do they manifest a strong, independent, anti-organization spirit? "And Moses sent to call Dathan and Abiram the sons of Eliab, but they said, 'We will not come up!'" (Numbers 16:12). Like these rebels of old, there are some today who have great difficulty submitting to the authority of the church. They will not be answerable to boards and committees. They will not take counsel from pastors and conference leaders. They flaunt the authority of the *Church Manual*. They not only behave as if they do not need the church; they behave as if they *are* the church.

"The spirit of pulling away from our fellow laborers, the spirit of disorganization, is in the very air we breathe. By some, all efforts to establish order are regarded as dangerous—as a restriction of personal liberty, and hence to be regarded as popery. They declare that they will not take any man's say-so; that they are amenable to no man. I have been instructed that it is Satan's special effort to lead men to feel that God is pleased to have them choose their own course, independent of the counsel of their brethren" (*Testimonies to Ministers and Gospel Workers*, pp. 488, 489).

Often church members have said to me, "But I find nothing wrong with anything they teach. It certainly rings true to my ears. In fact, they are teaching things that you seldom hear from our pulpits any more." Perhaps the question that should be asked is this: Do their teachings include what Seventh-day Adventists believe *about the church*?

It seems to seldom occur to our members to ask such a question, even though several of the twenty-eight fundamental beliefs have to do with the church. Why shouldn't alignment with those be just as important as the Sabbath and the Second Coming?

Do they lack balance? We must be careful here. Who among us is wholly consistent in what we teach and practice? Jesus encourages us to be attentive to heaven's smallest requirements but to make sure we do not lose sight of the "weightier matters of the law" (Matthew 23:23). It is, nonetheless, a common trait of splinter groups that their song is played on one or two strings. They have a great burden for health reform, for their brand of righteousness by faith, or for some aspect of Bible prophecy.

Dissident groups, who claim such high spiritual attainments, are often, along with some of us inside the church, plagued with glaring inconsistencies. They may pay close attention to diet but ignore their responsibilities in stewardship. They may be conscientious Sabbathkeepers but unnecessarily deprive their children of a Christian education.

Do they have a burden for soul-winning? Individuals involved in break-away groups typically are not good soul winners. The reasons are obvious.

First, they are typically antisocial toward anyone outside their own group, isolating themselves from others for fear of contamination. They do not imitate Jesus' example of mingling with "publicans and sinners." Their focus is inward, consumed with monitoring their own and others' behavior, and they have little energy or interest to invest in outreach to others.

Second, they look upon the church, not the world, as their mission field. Their "soul-winning" consists of bringing people out of the church into their camp. Since they have lost confidence in the church and are not active members of a local congregation, they have no place to bring new converts. Unhappy campers are not going to do well at promoting the joys of camping.

Third, they prize smallness. "There are little companies continually rising who believe that God is only with the very few, the very scattered, and their influence is to tear down and scatter that which God's servants build up" (*Testimonies for the Church*, vol. 1, p. 417). To people with this mindset, a church of a hundred or more members is a big church. They keep themselves small, thinking thereby to maintain their purity; but again, that mindset works to kill any enthusiasm for winning millions of the lost to Christ.

Do they ask you to support them with tithe and offerings, and are their financial records open to public scrutiny or at least available to donors? "And through covetousness shall they with feigned words make merchandise of you . . . following the way of Balaam the son of Bosor, who loved the wages of unrighteousness" (2 Peter 2:3, 15). Ellen White says there are "those who are . . . in opposition to organization, in opposition to the plain command of God spoken by Malachi in regard to bringing all the tithes into the treasury of God's house" (*Testimonies to Ministers and Gospel Workers*, p. 53).

Independent ministry groups have quibbled and strained over this "plain command of God" for years, hoping against hope to justify taking tithe from God's people and putting it in the "storehouse" of their own checking account. Ellen White defines the storehouse as "the treasury of God's house." God Himself defines the storehouse as "My house" (Malachi 3:10). How can that be any other than the recognized church organization?

We need to understand that there is a sense in which the tithe creates the church. Once we give someone our tithe, we have created a paid ministry, and that is foundational to the existence of any church. We have joined Korah, Dathan, and Abiram in attempting to make priests of those who are not qualified for the priesthood (Numbers 16:40). And those who accept tithe thereby acknowledge that they are a church separate from the Seventh-day Adventist church.

Many independent ministries will not submit to financial accountability, and yet they can be very critical of the way the church handles its money. Any church member, however, has the privilege of examining conference balance sheets. In that light, I have never understood why people will not give to the church where there are multiple levels of accountability, but they will give generously to some independent group that has no accountability to anyone! Anyone who donates to any cause has a right to receive financial statements upon request. Any person or organization that refuses such information should not be trusted.

Are they dishonest and secretive in their operations? Peter warned that "there will be false teachers among you, who will secretly bring in destructive heresies" (2 Peter 2:1). The church of God is not a secret society. Persons who give whispered invitations to clandestine meetings do not represent the openness and honesty that should characterize true Seventh-day Adventists. Individuals who arrange meetings without the knowledge of the local pastor and/or conference leaders should be viewed as disloyal conspirators.

"It will be found that those who bear false messages will not have a high sense of honor and integrity. They will deceive the people, and mix up with their error the *Testimonies* . . . They make such selections from the *Testimonies* as they think they can twist to support their positions, . . . so that their error may have weight and be accepted by the people" (*Testimonies to Ministers and Gospel Workers*, p. 42). "The Lord hates all deception, secrecy, and guile. This is Satan's work; the work of God is open and frank" (*Ibid*, p. 274).

Perhaps the most chilling description of the character and aims of these enemies that reside within as well as without the church is this: "The demon of heresy has mapped out the world, and has resolved to possess it as his kingdom. Those who are in his army are numerous. They are disguised, and are subtle and persevering. They resist every divine influence, and employ every instrumentality in order to compass the ruin of even one soul. They possess a zeal, tact, and ability that is marvelous, and press their way into every new opening where the standard of truth is uplifted" (*The Upward Look*, p. 275).

Well, what about the playful wolves on the left? Even though I have slanted the foregoing toward the breakaway, divisive elements of the far right, I would emphasize that you could ask many of these questions of those on the liberalizing, compromising left.

Can they, too, profess to have "new light"? Oh, yes! Especially "light" that makes light of obedience and strict conformity to the revealed will of God.

Do they find fault with church leadership? Yes, especially with those leaders with high standards whom they see as opposing their worldly lifestyles.

Do they lack balance? Without question.

Can they be secretive and dishonest in their operations? Definitely.

Are they guilty of dividing the church and creating a new kind of church? The evidence for that is overwhelming.[2]

Satan sees those in this camp as his very best allies. He says of them, "Those of this class who are apt and intelligent will serve as decoys to draw others into our snares. Many will not fear their influence, because they profess the same faith. [Notice now how precisely Satan states both their essential theology and their mission.] We will thus lead them to conclude that the requirements of Christ are less strict than they once believed, and that by conformity to the world they would exert a greater influence with worldlings" (*Testimonies to Ministers and Gospel Workers*, p. 474).

Whether right or left, we are challenged to be kind and courteous to all of these dear people—kind but cautious; loving but wise; gentle but firm. "They are to be met and opposed, not because they are bad men, but because they are teachers of falsehood and are endeavoring to put upon falsehood the stamp of truth" (*Testimonies to Ministers and Gospel Workers*, p. 55). Prodigals do come home. It is not our place to judge any as hopeless. It *is* our place to be watchful and firm in protecting ourselves and our fellow believers from predators who would make raids upon God's flock.

And right now might be a good time to check our own willingness to submit to the authority and guidance of the church.

Some Wolves Wear Wool Suits

Discussion Questions:

1. Is my local church providing sufficient opportunity for our members to be grounded in Bible truth?
2. Are the members of my local congregation more susceptible to deceptions coming from the right or from the left? What are some of those deceptions?
3. Do you agree that "the tithe creates the church"?
4. Do you agree that those with theological views differing from those held by the church should submit those views to "brethren of experience"? If the "brethren" decide against them, what should they do?
5. Are you and the members of your congregation excited by the reports of the advance of the gospel around the world? If not, what can you do to change that?
6. Is your church more at risk from negative influences from break-away groups on the far right or from those of the liberalizing left? What is your church doing to protect its members from either or both of these?

Endnotes

1 Clifford Goldstein, *The Remnant* (Boise: Pacific Press Publishing Association, 1994), 119. *(The full force of this statement can be appreciated by the reader only if it is remembered that Goldstein is Jewish and that this was written when Saddam Hussein was at the height of his power in Iraq.)*
2 There are probably as many or more such independent, congregational-style churches that represent the liberal left than there are that cater to the far right. Such churches often hold two separate worship services—one for "traditional" worshipers, and another for those who want a "contemporary" style. In so doing, they stay under the umbrella of the organized church and escape being labeled as separationist.

Chapter Ten

EVERYONE SUBMITS

"Submitting to one another in the fear of God" (Ephesians 5:21).

"Likewise you younger people submit to your elders. Yes, all of you be submissive to one another, and be clothed with humility" (1 Peter 5:5).

When my brothers and I were in our teens, we used to test our strength by facing each other, lacing our fingers together, and then trying to force the other one to kneel. After I got married, I decided to try the same thing with my wife. (I missed my brothers.) But even though I exerted great pressure and kept repeating the words "Kneel! Kneel!" she would not kneel! Eventually, I became ashamed of myself and gave up. And then, believe it or not, she scolded me for hurting her fingers.

"All you had to do was kneel," I said. I learned that feminine stubbornness and pride will endure a lot of pain rather than submit!

We are a society schooled in winning, not submitting. We question every call by the umpire. We challenge election results. We fight to protect our rights. We guard against the intrusion of government. And submitting to the authority of the church may be the hardest of all. But, rather than try to be discreet, I'm going to put the bottom line right here at the top: Our ties to the church are no stronger than the authority we permit it to have over us.

We tend to view our relationship to the church as that of a volunteer. We joined of our own volition and serve at our pleasure. The idea that the church can exercise authority that would in any way limit our personal freedom and independence is not always welcome. In fact, we may view such exercise of authority as both anti-American

Everyone Submits

and anti-Christian. We demand religious liberty within the church, not fully accepting the fact that, to a very large degree, we surrendered that liberty in the very act of exercising it.

Suppose I enlist in the US Army but refuse to wear the uniform and insist on living at home and following my own schedule. "Ridiculous," you say. "You made a choice; you cannot be soldier and civilian at the same time."

But can I be member and non-member at the same time? Can I enjoy the privileges and benefits of belonging while spurning its authority? More seriously, can the Seventh-day Adventist church complete its mission without system and order, without leaders who lead and followers who submit to leadership?

It's hard to submit; but God, in His Word, has plainly asked us to do just that. He insists upon it. "All of you be submissive to one another" (1 Peter 5:5). But isn't that dangerous? Submitting to God, we understand, but submitting to one another? "One another" can take in a lot of strange people! And that challenges us to find the balance point between being too submissive and too independent; between being a doormat and a stubborn mule; between being a Mr. Milktoast and an ornery nut that is crossthreaded with everyone else.

First of all, the Bible makes it clear that everyone submits. Ephesians 5:21 is the umbrella under which Paul fits all the rest—"submitting to one another in the fear of God." Even though the word "submit" is not used in each case that is Paul's clear intent. Wives submit to their husbands as they submit to Christ (verses 22-24); husbands submit to their wives by loving them as Christ loves the Church (verses 25-33). Children submit in loving obedience to their parents (Ephesians 6:1-3); parents submit by putting the welfare of their children ahead of their own, training them for the Lord (verse 4). Employees submit in that they work for their boss as faithfully as if they were working for Christ (verses 5-8); and employers submit by treating their employees as Christ would treat them (verse 9).

God is fair. The command takes in all. There is no executive privilege. No one climbs to such a high position that he no longer washes feet. No one is excused because it's too hard. No one can beg off because he was born with a surplus of natural independence.

Second, we need to define what it means to submit to one another "in the fear of God." Most of us grew up hearing mission stories about people, usually children and wives, who would not submit to an enraged father and husband who demanded that they violate their consciences. Often they were severely beaten and disowned because of their faithfulness in keeping the Sabbath. Even as a very young Christian I understood that I was not required to submit in violation of conscience, not even to my own parents. The words "in the fear of God" stake out some boundaries to our required submission. Like the young Hebrews standing before the king's idol on the plain of Dura, there are times when we have to say, "We will not kneel!"

Having established those two points, we can now explore what it means to submit to one another in the church.

We submit to the authority of the church because it is an agency through which Christ exercises His authority. If we are going to submit to the church, we must understand the nature, source, and proper exercise of its authority. "As Creator, Redeemer and Sustainer, Lord and King of all creation, God alone is the source and ground of authority for the church."[1] The church's authority is a delegated authority; it is not designed by man, nor can it be self-assumed. God gave authority to His prophets and apostles (2 Corinthians 10:8), and their words are still the basis of the church's authority today. In the early church, elders and bishops were given authority to carry out their leadership functions (Acts 20:17-28). They had authority to decide what was sound doctrine and what was error (1 Timothy 3:1, 2). The entire church body was held accountable for purity of doctrine and discipline of its members (1 John 4:1; 1 Thessalonians 5:21). Questions of concern to the whole church were decided by a general council (Acts 15:6-35).

From their beginning, Seventh-day Adventists have attempted to follow the New Testament model and have developed a representative form of church government. Just as the decisions of the Jerusalem Council (Acts 6:2; 8:14) were not made by vote of every member of the church, so not every member votes on every church issue at every level of the organization today.

"Every member of the church has a voice in choosing officers of the church. The church chooses the officers of the state conferences. Delegates chosen by the state conferences choose the officers of the union conferences; and delegates chosen by the union conferences choose the officers of the General Conference. By this arrangement every conference, every institution, every church, and every individual, either directly or through representatives, has a voice in the election of the men who bear the chief responsibilities in the General Conference" (*Testimonies for the Church*, vol. 8, pp. 236, 237).

The Seventh-day Adventist church is God's church, but the human element is not perfect. Mistakes can be made at all levels. There is one body, however, to whose decisions we are especially advised to submit—those of the delegates to a General Conference session. "I have been shown that no man's judgment should be surrendered to the judgment of any one man. But when the judgment of the General Conference, which is the highest authority that God has upon the earth, is exercised, private independence and private judgment must not be maintained, but be surrendered" (*Testimonies for the Church*, vol. 3, p. 492).

Why are the decisions of the General Conference to be trusted? Because they reflect "the judgment of the brethren assembled from all parts of the field" (*Testimonies for the Church*, vol. 9, p. 260). I have attended a General Conference session and marveled at the wisdom of the decisions made after thorough debate, and after being filtered through the minds of delegates from North

America, Indonesia, India, Africa, Europe, South America, and other parts of the world. I came away convinced that the Spirit of God was present and working to protect His people from heresy and division.

Those decisions made at General Conference sessions that impact members at the local level are communicated through the various editions of The Church Manual. "The Church Manual is the expression of the Seventh-day Adventist Church's understanding of Christian life and church governance and discipline based on biblical principles" (*The Church Manual*, 2000 edition, p. 2). It is easy to say that we believe it is God's church because it holds to the pure doctrines of the Bible; difficulties arise when we move into those areas of policy and procedure that are not overtly doctrinal and/or Bible-based. We feel at liberty to contest those rules of the church that deal with discipline, church finance, qualifications for holding office, etc.

During my service as a district pastor, I occasionally had a member object to being guided by policies spelled out in The Church Manual. "Those are man's rules!" was the cry of protest. Let's test the logic of that charge. If Christ has nothing to do with the formulation of the church's operational policies; if, in fact, He absents Himself from General Conference sessions when policies crucial to the unity and prosperity of the church are being voted, allowing the outcome to be wholly human, can He, in truth, claim to be the Head of the church (Ephesians 5:23)? If I have the privilege of deciding that some policies are wholly human, I have the power to make ineffective the church's authority and my obligation to submit to it.

We are to submit to the counsel and guidance of the church unless it can be shown that such counsel is in clear contradiction to the Word of God. "He who despises the authority of the church despises the authority of Christ Himself" (*Desire of Ages*, p. 805). "God has invested His church with special authority and power which no one can be justified in disregarding and despising, for in so doing he despises the voice of God" (*Testimonies for the Church*, vol. 3, p. 417).

Pretty strong words! But God has not left us without reason to exercise such trust. Writing to a man who was struggling to submit to church authority, Ellen White said, "You should have submitted to the judgment of the church. If they decided wrong, God could take hold of this matter in His own time and vindicate the right. He does not lay upon you the responsibility of keeping the church in order" (*Manuscript Releases*, vol. 5, p. 297).

I don't believe that counsel sets aside, in the least, all that has been said about protesting the wrongs in the church. It means that there comes a time when, after we have stated our position, we submit to the judgment of the church, if we can conscientiously do so, when due process has been followed. Then we trust God to manage the church and, in His own time, correct those things that need correcting.

We submit to the voice of the majority. God never asks us to submit to one man's mind or one person's judgment, even if that one person is the oldest, wealthiest, or most articulate person in the congregation—and not even if that one man is the pastor or the conference president. Nor are we asked to submit to any group that might be formed to promote its own agenda. The Seventh-day Adventist church, at all levels of its organization, operates by majority vote, and each member is expected to set aside his or her private opinion and support the majority unless, as we have said, it can be shown that those decisions violate the law of God.

"The church is God's delegated authority upon earth. . . . It is the want of deference for the opinions of the church that causes so much trouble among brethren. . . . The majority of the church is a power which should control its individual members. . . . Unless the advice and counsel of the church can be respected, it is indeed powerless. God has placed a voice in the church which must control its members" (*Testimonies for the Church*, vol. 5, p. 107).

Let me give you an example. The question of whether or not to build a large addition to a church where I was pastor was being discussed at a business meeting. A leading layman vigorously opposed the project. Finally, a motion was made to move forward, and it carried by a wide margin. Immediately, the dissenter rose to his feet and walked out, giving his fellow members a clear message that he would not submit to their judgment.

Let me tell you what this good man could have done. I was a delegate to a conference constituency meeting during which a project costing several hundred thousand dollars was proposed. One of the delegates went to the microphone and spoke for several minutes in strong opposition to the project, but when it was brought to a vote, at least 90 percent of the delegates voted in favor. To my great surprise and delight, I learned later that the delegate who had opposed the action so emphatically had, before he left the place of meeting, handed the conference president a check for several thousand dollars to be used toward the very project he had spoken against.

That is the model we should emulate. We meet together, we discuss, we appoint committees, and eventually we vote. And, like the delegate just mentioned, we show our submission to the authority of the church by cheerfully and generously supporting even the very things we voted against. Anyone who can do that is surely not far from the kingdom!

We submit to the church's right to direct the mission of the church. The gospel commission has been given to the church and it is expected that its individual members will work unitedly to fulfill that mission. Each member has the privilege of seeking God's direction in assessing and employing his or her gifts, but the exercise of those gifts must also be subject to the judgment of the church body. That is done, not to shackle a willing worker, but to maximize the efficient use of the church's human and material resources.

The proliferation of private ministries has been a blessing to the church for the most part, but has also, to some degree, been problematic. Many of these ministries obtain tax exempt status, publish a newsletter, and seek to build a financial base among Adventist members. This can have the effect, not only of weakening the church's ability to fund its own ministries, but even to stay in control of its mission and identity in the world. We have some in our midst who are under the delusion that they are divinely called to do such and such a work, needed or not, wanted or not, ready or not. There's plenty of room for every willing worker, but all need to work closely with church leadership to make sure they really are making a contribution to the overall mission of the church.

We submit to each other's gifts. The authority of the church is exercised largely through the spiritual gifts that have been distributed to its members. Through the election process, members are given offices where they are to exercise those gifts. It behooves every member, then, to honor that selection by submitting to the authority inherent in those offices. We may feel that we or someone else could do a better job, but it is a serious abuse of church authority to ignore, bypass, or belittle those who are conscientiously trying to fulfill their offices.

It may help to remind ourselves often that these are spiritual gifts. They contribute to the spiritual life of the church. They are what make the church work. The Sabbath School superintendent, the head deacon, the personal ministries leader, and all the rest need to know that we submit to the rightful exercise of their church office. The goal of each congregation should be to elect those they trust and then trust those they elect.

We submit to pastoral leadership. Even though she had much to say about "kingly power" and the abuse of authority, Ellen White urged church members to be respectful of their ministers. "God has bestowed power on the church and the ministers of the church, and it is not a light matter to resist the authority and despise the judgment of God's ministers" (*Manuscript Releases*, vol. 5, p. 297).

Pastors have had special training and experience in church leadership and are usually in a position to see the bigger picture. They have been set apart by ordination to perform a sacred ministry. They are to be seen as God's spokesmen. "Reveal to all you associate with that you regard the message from God's servants as a message to you from God Himself" (*Testimonies for the Church*, vol. 5, p. 498). That may require a bit of editing at times, but it is the only attitude to take to church.

We submit to the church's authority to formulate doctrine. This is in harmony with what has already been said about the authority of the delegates to a General Conference session. Through a process of delegated authority, the church has enunciated its doctrinal positions in twenty-eight statements of fundamental beliefs. This does not contradict its strong encouragement for each member to search the Scriptures. "The Seventh-day Adventist Statement of Fundamental Beliefs does not in any way take away from the authority or supremacy of the Bible. Rather, the fact that the church has taken a definite stand on certain biblical fundamental beliefs reflects its responsible commitment to the sol scriptura principle and its continuing trust in the Bible as the inspired Word of God." [2]

But what if individual members, believing they are Spirit-led, arrive at different conclusions? Who decides which conclusion, if any, is correct? The church does. This is perhaps the greatest challenge to some members' independence. But what are the options? To allow individuals, churches, or even divisions to operate on any other base would be to capitulate to congregationalism—to become so fragmented as to become meaningless.

And what if, over time, the church's decision turns out to be wrong? We can conjecture endlessly about such "what ifs." To such questions, I know of no substitute for trusting Christ's leadership of the church. If it is the "one object on earth upon which He bestows in a special sense His love and regard" ("The Church of God," *Review and*

Herald, December 4, 1900), He is not going to let it go far adrift doctrinally.

We submit to the church's authority to discipline its members. In his book *Stop Dating the Church,* Joshua Harris gives the reader ten questions to ask before choosing a church. Perhaps the most arresting is this: "Is this a church that is willing to kick me out?"[3] His point is that a church that has no rules, or doesn't enforce the ones they have, is not worth considering.

"Let none speak lightly of the duty of the church to administer censure and rebuke; neither let them criticize the action of the church when this painful task becomes necessary.... God has commanded that those who prove themselves unworthy of church fellowship shall be separated from His body. Those who speak against the exercise of this authority speak against the authority of Christ" (*Manuscript Releases,* vol. 17, p. 164).

"Sin and sinners in the church must be promptly dealt with, that others may not be contaminated. Truth and purity require that we make more thorough work to cleanse the camp from Achans. Let those in responsible positions not suffer sin in a brother. Show him that he must either put away his sins or be separated from the church" (*Testimonies for the Church,* vol. 5, p. 147).

But what if the local church fails to discipline its members, allowing the whole congregation to come under the frown of God? The organized church has made provision for such a crisis. A local church may be dissolved or expelled from the conference organization; that is, the majority of the delegates to a conference constituency meeting may vote to close the church and drop its offending members from membership (See *The Church Manual,* 2000 edition, pp. 201-204).

The exercise of church authority and the administering of church discipline are to be expressions of love. It is that kind of love that leads us to hold each other accountable—the kind of love that can get beyond the vagaries of human emotion and do what is best for the body of Christ.

The Church That Does Not Fall

Our attitude toward submission to the authority of the church is closely linked to our view of how church membership relates to our salvation. Let's go there next.

Discussion Questions:
1. Do you agree that a person surrenders certain rights when he or she joins the church? Give examples.
2. Describe the difference in the source of authority for the Seventh-day Adventist church and that of an independent community church.
3. Does your local congregation operate by majority rule? Could it do better?
4. Are you satisfied with the way your local church handles discipline? What, if anything, needs to change?
5. Do you feel the Adventist church's method of maintaining doctrinal unity is working well? Why or why not?

Endnotes

1 *Seventh-day Adventist Church Manual* (Hagerstown: Review and Herald Publishing Association, 2000), 1.
2 Kwabena Donkor, "The Role of the Statement of Beliefs and Creeds," *Journal of the Adventist Theological Society* (Spring 2007): 101.
3 Joshua Harris, *Stop Dating the Church* (Sisters: Multnomah Publishers, 2004), 93.

Chapter Eleven

THE CHURCH AND MY SALVATION

"And the Lord added to the church daily those who were being saved" (Acts 2:47).

Jesus sits by Jacob's well in the glaring noontide heat. He watches as a lone woman comes through the gate of the nearby village and walks slowly down the path toward the well, her water jar balanced on her head. He wonders what circumstance brings her on her errand at this unusual hour. Shortly she arrives and, pretending not to notice the Man seated nearby, sets her pot on the stone pavement and begins to fasten the rope to it.

"Give Me a drink," Jesus says.

The startled woman straightens and looks at Him. "How is it that You, being a Jew, ask a drink from me, a Samaritan woman?" (John 4:9).

The conversation turns to a discussion of well water and living water and then to the woman's private life. Becoming more and more uncomfortable, she tries to steer the conversation toward the right place to worship. Pointing to Mt. Gerizim, she says, "Our fathers worshiped on this mountain, but you Jews say that in Jerusalem is the place where one ought to worship" (verse 20).

Jesus replies, "You worship what you do not know; we know what we worship, for salvation is of the Jews" (verse 22).

Salvation is of the Jews? Why would He say that? In a few months He will make the startling announcement to the Jewish leaders, "Your house is left to you desolate" (Matthew 23:38). And shortly thereafter they will instigate His crucifixion. Surely, at this point in history, Israel cannot be the place to find salvation!

But Jesus here affirms what the Old Testament has taught throughout its pages: *Whatever the spiritual con-*

dition of its members in any given time and place, God's church is still the best place to find one's way to God. That has always been the meaning and purpose of "church" as God defines it. When that church was Israel, if a Syrian or Samaritan or Egyptian wanted to have a relationship with the true God and be involved in true worship, he had only one choice: join himself to Israel.

The Samaritans had tried to start their own church—a mixture of paganism and Judaism. And so Jesus, the Jew, reminds this woman, the Samaritan, that "salvation is of the Jews." It was as if He was saying, "We have the truth; you are in error. God has chosen Mt. Zion, not Mt. Gerizim. You are worshiping in the wrong place."

Is that still true today? Can it be said that obtaining salvation involves finding the right church and holding membership in that church, no matter what its spiritual condition might be? I think it might help to ask the question this way: *"In God's plan, how does connection with God's church contribute to my salvation?"* I have listed several ways in which those two work together.

Baptism seals my commitment to Jesus and automatically unites me with His church. I hear someone saying, "Baptism doesn't save me; church membership doesn't save me; Jesus saves me." My answer: "Baptism into church membership is Jesus' *way* of saving you." I have found no Bible or Spirit of Prophecy support for the practice of being "baptized into Christ" without uniting with the church. The thousands that joined the church following Pentecost did so by baptism (Acts 2:38-41). Jesus' parting words to His disciples were, "He that believes and is baptized will be saved" (Mark 16:16). I have no choice. If I am able to do so, I must be baptized to meet heaven's entrance requirements.

God's messenger affirms this point: "Christ has made baptism the sign of entrance to His spiritual kingdom. He has made this a positive condition with which all must comply who wish to be acknowledged as under the authority of the Father, the Son, and the Holy Spirit. Before man can find a home in the church, before passing the threshold of God's spiritual kingdom, he is to receive [through baptism] the impress of the divine name, 'The Lord our Righteousness.' Jeremiah 23:6." (*Testimonies for the Church*, vol. 6, p. 91).

"The Father, the Son, and the Holy Ghost, powers infinite and omniscient, receive those who truly enter into covenant relation with God. They are present at every baptism, to receive the candidates who have renounced the world and have received Christ into the soul temple. These candidates have entered into the family of God, and their names are inscribed in the Lamb's book of life" (*God's Amazing Grace*, p. 143).

While we will readily agree that "it is the character, not the placing of our names on the church books, that makes us Christians" (*The Upward Look*, p. 28), listen to what Ellen White says church membership means. "Those who place their names on the church book should do so with a full and intelligent understanding of what this action involves.

- *It means* that you have solemnly pledged yourself to serve God.
- *It means* that you have made a full surrender of self to Him, in order that Christ may reign where self once reigned.
- *It means* that you have given up your pet ideas and policies, and have yielded your mind to the mind of Christ.
- *It means* that your fixed purpose is to be one with God, one with His people;
- [*It means*] that you will exercise self-denial and self-sacrifice to advance the interests of His kingdom;
- [*It means*] that you will strive to overcome everything that hinders growth in grace" (*The Upward Look*, p. 143, [formatting and italics mine]).

The church's part is to help me remember my baptismal covenant and live in harmony with those solemn pledges. The church that taught me "present truth" is the best place for me to continue to grow in the knowledge and practice of that truth and to be held accountable for keeping my baptismal vows. I need to be continually enrolled in refresher courses. And the church is God's ordained agency for offering those courses through Sabbath School classes, evangelistic meetings, preaching services, and a host of seminars. Unattached to the church, I can quickly become a law unto myself, thinking that I am right when I have drifted far off course.

My identity with the church helps to keep me from being re-assimilated into the world. To decide in favor of church membership is to make a clear statement about my identity. I am now a "member of the household of God" (Ephesians 2:19). Identity is a powerful thing. When Americans travel abroad, it is not uncommon for them to use their identity to gain protection and privileges that might not be as readily granted to others. My identity and affiliation with the church may not be the best reason for living a life that honors Christ, but it can be a significant factor in helping me to do that. When tempted to be lax, I remember: "The world is watching Seventh-day Adventists because it knows something of their profession of faith and of their high standard, and when it sees those who do not live up to their profession, it points at them with scorn" (*Testimonies for the Church*, vol. 9, p. 23). But if I am not a member, what reason do I have to be concerned about the church's reputation?

God intends that His people today stand in the same relationship to the world that His people Israel did in the Old Testament period. Their distinctive differences were to keep them from assimilating with the pagan nations surrounding them. God gave them strict marriage laws, dress laws, health laws, worship laws, tithe and offering laws, family discipline laws—all to make it very difficult for them to be assimilated into any other society.

Having said all this, we must point out that there is a separateness that protects and an exclusiveness that corrupts. Our position is to be far from the world in spirit

My Church and My Salvation

and lifestyle, but close to the world in compassion. We are in the world but not of the world. We are in but not of. Like a boat in the water—that's where boats are meant to be. Problems develop when water gets into the boat.

Connection with the church helps me grow in my appreciation for sacred things and keep the sacred and the common properly separated. The line that separates the sacred and the common is all too easily crossed. The church is a holy place and my going into its precincts at least once or twice a week helps me reflect on the holiness of God and the true meaning of worship. "The Lord is in His holy temple. Let all the earth keep silence before Him" (Habakkuk 2:20). There I place myself under the pillar of cloud, as it were, and move through my workaday week with an outlook that is a bit less secular and calloused, and a bit more reverent than it might have been otherwise.

"God is high and holy; and to the humble, believing soul, His house on earth, the place where His people meet for worship, is as the gate of heaven. The song of praise, the words spoken by Christ's ministers, are God's appointed agencies to prepare a people for the church above" (*The Faith I Live By*, p. 188).

The church contributes to my salvation by putting me to work for the salvation of others. The church assesses its own needs and those of its community and tries to match those with the spiritual gifts of its members. Millions of people have become active Christian workers because the church set them to work.

"Every church should be a training school for Christian workers. Its members should be taught how to give Bible readings, how to conduct and teach Sabbath School classes, how best to help the poor and to care for the sick, how to work for the unconverted. . . . There should not only be teaching, but actual work under experienced instructors" (*Christian Service*, p. 59).

My connection with the church gives me opportunity to be trained and employed in outreach and also keeps me informed about the progress of the work locally and around the world. As I see the tremendous progress of the three angels' messages, I am inspired to do my part, to work harder, and to sacrifice more. I am grateful to be part of a movement so apparently led by God.

Believe it or not, the odds in favor of my salvation are improved because the church gives me a sense of history. The Jews loved to remind everyone that they served the God of Abraham, Isaac, and Jacob. It gave them a strong sense of belonging. A line from the song of Moses says, "Remember the days of old, consider the years of many generations. Ask your father, and he will show you; your elders, and they will tell you" (Deuteronomy 32:7).

We, too, will find that keeping in touch with our spiritual ancestors—people like William Miller, Joseph Bates, James and Ellen White, Uriah and Annie Smith, J. N. Andrews, S. N. Haskell, J. N. Loughborough—will strengthen our attachment to the Lord and to His church. As we relive the trials and triumphs of those early days, we are able to say with some satisfaction, "Those are my people." We walk where they walked, kneel where they knelt, and we face the world stronger.

We need to experience, in part at least, the sense of exhilaration that Ellen White felt when she wrote, "As I see what the Lord has wrought, I am filled with astonishment, and with confidence in Christ as leader. We have nothing to fear for the future, except as we shall forget the way the Lord has led us, and His teaching in our past history" (*Last Day Events*, p. 72). When everything is shaking that can be shaken, who knows, the memory of how God has led His people in the past might be the very thing that gives us that extra bit of courage to hang on.

Our own personal history in the church also creates powerful bonds that help hold us on course. Church school, academy, and college classmates, Sabbath School teachers, camp meeting memories, older members who took us under their wings—all these and more become "accountability partners," as it were, that keep us headed the right direction.

My Church and My Salvation

The church is the "tumbler" where I receive the polish I need for citizenship in heaven. As an amateur rock hound, I enjoy finding rough, unattractive rocks in some mountain or desert location, bringing them home, and putting them in a tumbler where they are changed into beautiful, glossy "gems." In similar fashion, my association with others in the church can have a refining effect on the roughness in my character. Outside of the church, I can do my own thing and avoid people I would just as soon not come in contact with. But in the church, if I'm involved at all, I will experience bumps and scrapes that put the mettle of my character to the test. "By mutual contact minds receive polish and refinement" (*The Adventist Home*, p. 547).

Connection with the church strengthens my connection with Christ. Paul says "Christ is the head of the church, and He is the *Savior* of the body" (Ephesians 5:23). The plan of salvation places us in the church under the headship of Christ, the most secure place in the world for those being saved. Ellen White confirms it: "Very close and sacred is the relation between Christ and His church—He the bridegroom and the church the bride; He the head, and the church the body. Connection with Christ, then, involves connection with His church" (*Education*, p. 268). The English language could not be plainer.

"In the ministry of Christ and His apostles, those who were converted to the truth were brought into church relationship; and every stray, lost sheep that was found, was brought to the fold of the church, that under the direction of the Master, through the undershepherds, they might go in and out and find pasture" ("Sanctification," *Signs of the Times*, October 23, 1879).

It will not do for me to say I have a relationship with Christ, and that's all that matters. "Many have an idea that they are responsible to Christ alone for their light and experience, independent of His recognized followers on earth. . . . but He respects the means that He has ordained for the enlightenment and salvation of men;

He directs sinners to the church, which He has made a channel of light to the world" (*The Acts of the Apostles*, p. 122).

The most positive connection between the church and the believer's salvation is found in the very first sentence in the book *The Acts of the Apostles*: "The church is God's appointed agency for the salvation of men" (p. 9). Typically, a person's introduction to Christ has come through some agency of the church, so joining the church is the logical next step. In any case, it is always God's plan that a person's connection with Christ will, in due course, also connect that individual to His church. A person may meet and accept Christ as his Savior *before* he knows about the church, but as we have noted before, it is Jesus' desire that all of His sheep be gathered into one fold.

The church is the only place to be when Jesus comes. Hundreds say it, and perhaps thousands think it: "I'm just as good as those who go to church." I don't know of anyone who could dispute that. There are people in the church who are pretty bad. And there are people in the world who seem to be caring, kind, and honest.

But there are two things wrong with the "just-as-good-as" argument. First, our goodness does not save us; the righteousness of Christ does. When Jesus comes, whether you and I are seated in church, in prison, or hiding in a mountain cave, we will not be caught up to meet Him in the air because of our goodness. It will be because we have been justified and sanctified by His goodness.

Second, when Jesus comes looking for His people, He expects to find them in the one fold that He has identified as His. If we want the destroying angel to pass over, we must be in the one place where His blood is over the lintel of the door—"the church of God which He purchased with His own blood" (Acts 20:28)—even if that church has been driven into the wilderness. Will God's people still be found in all churches or outside any church when Jesus comes? No. When the call to come out of Babylon is finished, the days of the scattered church will be over. All the sheep will be in one fold.

My Church and My Salvation

So, have we answered the question? Is church membership required for salvation? Try this question: Will good works save me? If you answer correctly, you will say, "No, good works will not save me, but I cannot be saved without good works" (See *Selected Messages*, bk. 1, p. 377). The same apparent paradox fits the question about church membership and salvation.

Will church membership save me? If we answer correctly, we will say, "No, church membership will not save me, but if God has invited me to join His last-day remnant church, I cannot be saved outside of it."

It seems foolish even to consider anything else. The church is an integral part of God's plan for saving us. To ignore that plan or rebel against it could cost us eternal life. To join the church on earth is to join the church in heaven.

Can these bold assertions be supported by Jesus' example? That's next.

Discussion Questions:

1. Of all the arguments presented in this chapter that show that church membership is part of God's plan for saving us, which would you rate as most effective in your experience?
2. Why is being "baptized into Christ," but not into the church, not acceptable? What are the reasons some people might give for doing that?
3. God has given the Seventh-day Adventist church high standards to keep its members from being assimilated into the world. Is that working well? If not, why not?
4. Has your local church done a good job of putting its members to work for others?
5. In your own words, how would you answer the question: "Is church membership required for salvation?"

Chapter Twelve

WAS JESUS A GOOD CHURCH MEMBER?

"And as His custom was, He went into the synagogue on the Sabbath day, and stood up to read" (Luke 4:16).

Jesus a good church member? It seems a bit irreverent even to pose the question. It could imply that Jesus came short of being the perfect example for His followers. I can assure you, I do not intend to challenge the perfection of our Savior. Jesus is the best of all that is good. What I will challenge is our *misconceptions* about His relationship to the church in His day and ours.

It seems to be widely believed that Jesus had a rather distant relationship to the church. People are quick to point out that Jesus was often in conflict with church leadership—the infamous "scribes and Pharisees" of His day. We are often reminded that it was the leaders of the organized church that rejected and crucified Him. So if Jesus didn't have much use for organized religion, aren't His followers justified in sharing that distrust?

This is an age of cynicism and suspicion. We might call it the "anti" age. People are increasingly anti-government, anti-business, anti-media, anti-conformity, and anti-church. Of course, that cynicism is not wholly groundless. Heaven knows how graphically and routinely our political and business leaders have disappointed us, how even church leaders have been found to have feet of clay. We have learned the truth of the Scripture that says, "Do not put your trust in princes, nor in a son of man, in whom there is no help" (Psalm 146:3).

But when it comes to the church, I believe a case can be made for making a difference. In Ephesians 2:19-20, Paul speaks of the "members of the household of God [the church]" as "having been built on the foundation of the apostles and prophets, Jesus Christ Himself being the chief cornerstone." The church has a divine element that sets it apart and above every human institution. The church is composed of fallible people, but it follows an infallible Leader. I believe Jesus has shown us how to relate to such a church. Let's look at the Bible evidence.

First, there is evidence that Jesus grew up in a home where the institution we call the organized church was honored by His parents and that they and He benefited from the services it provided. In Luke 2:22-24, we read: "Now when the days of her [Mary's] purification <u>according to the law of Moses</u> [Leviticus 12:2-8] were completed, they brought Him to Jerusalem to present Him to the Lord (<u>as it is written in the law of the Lord</u>, *'Every male who opens the womb shall be called holy to the Lord'*), and to offer a sacrifice <u>according to what is said in the law of the Lord</u>, *'A pair of turtledoves or two young pigeons.'*"

"And when the parents brought in the Child Jesus, to do for Him <u>according to the custom of the law</u>, he [Simeon] took Him up in his arms and blessed God" (verse 27).

"So when they had <u>performed all things according to the law of the Lord</u>, they returned to Galilee, to their own city, Nazareth" (verse 39). . . . "And when He was twelve years old, they went up to Jerusalem <u>according to the custom of the feast</u>" (verse 42).

The italics are original in the foregoing texts, but I added the underscoring to emphasize how often Luke reminds his readers that Jesus' parents are complying with "the law of the Lord." They are not slavishly following some rabbinical code; they are conforming to the instructions Jesus Himself had given His people through Moses. The child Jesus is not shielded from Old Testament church ritual; rather, virtually from the moment He is born, He is placed in a position to receive the blessings available through the services of the church.

In fact, His parents' compliance with the prescribed rituals turned out to be a series of divine appointments foreordained by His heavenly Father. Luke says that

The Church That Does Not Fall

Simeon came "by the Spirit into the temple" (Luke 2:27). The Holy Spirit impressed him to enter the temple at that very moment in order to connect with Jesus and His parents. What if Jesus' parents had not been there? What if Joseph had said to Mary, "We don't have to go by the 'church manual'; those are man's rules. Let's go back to Nazareth. We can dedicate our baby ourselves." Would Simeon have seen the Lord's Christ before his death and given public testimony to His divinity?

Also, in Luke 2:36-38, we read of Anna, a prophetess, who, coming to the temple "that instant," recognized the infant Jesus as the Messiah and declared, with the authority of the gift of prophecy, who He was. In fact, it says she "spoke of Him to all those who looked for redemption in Jerusalem." Pretty amazing! For days, this dear lady kept reminding people that prophecy had been fulfilled. What seemed like routine church obligations were divine appointments of great significance!

And here is the application we can make in our own relationship to the church today: One reason God brought the church into existence was to perform important services for its members through its teaching, preaching, and health ministries; its baptismal, communion, funeral, wedding, child dedication, education, and publishing services. Those services play a significant role in the spiritual health of each of us.

I have met those who feel that they and others who are likeminded can perform all those services for themselves. My answer is that, in America at least, you are free to do that. And in so doing you have created your own church. But please do not pretend it is a Seventh-day Adventist church or a part of the remnant. That church was called into existence beginning back in 1844. You cannot create what already exists.

Let's be honest and recognize that Jesus created and organized the church to provide services for His followers that cannot be provided by the family or any entity outside the church. He invites us to enjoy those privileges and blessings. That's what He and His parents did.

Second, Jesus set us an example in church attendance. In Luke 4:16 we read the familiar text: "And as His custom was, He went to the synagogue on the Sabbath day." "As His *custom* was." Those whose memories go back four or five decades may remember a time when it was customary for nearly every able-bodied Seventh-day Adventist to go to church on the Sabbath. We seldom thought of doing anything else. But what a novel idea *regular* church attendance is today! Most churches are fortunate to have 50 percent of their members attending on any given Sabbath. Half of us stay home or gad about. We need to recognize that for what it is: cruel and unjust treatment of those who are faithful, those who have to do double or triple duty—both in leadership and financial support—because of our absence.

I often hear people express their desire to have been with Jesus during His earthly ministry—to walk with Him, listen to Him, and witness the joy of those healed by His touch. But what if you had a job that kept you away from Him during the week? As a child, as a teen, and as an adult, Jesus was found in the local synagogue in Nazareth each Sabbath, seated with His parents, brothers, and sisters—week after week for thirty years![1] That is where you would have found Him then, and that is still where we will find Him every Sabbath morning.

Like Jesus, we need to make church attendance our *customary* practice. We need to stop worrying about who's preaching, having special music, or teaching the Sabbath School class. Jesus did not go to church just to hear a sermon. After all, at age twelve He had a better understanding of the Scriptures than the Ph.D.'s in Jerusalem. Jesus went to church because that's where God meets with His people.

And please don't miss this: The Scripture says He went to the synagogue. He went to the recognized, specified, God-ordained place of meeting. He went to the place dedicated to the worship of God. And He didn't stay away because bad people came to church. According to Nathanael, that's about the only kind there were in Nazareth (John 1:46).

Third, Jesus took part in worship services. At the beginning of Jesus' ministry in the Nazareth synagogue, He "stood up to read" (Luke 4:16). Was that also customary for Him? Yes. Speaking of His years as a youth and young adult, Ellen White writes, "And often in the synagogue on the Sabbath day He was called upon to read the lesson from the prophets, and the hearts of the hearers thrilled as a new light shone out from the familiar words of the sacred text" (*The Desire of* Ages, p. 74).

It certainly would have seemed out of character for Him to attend church just as a spectator. The habit of participating in worship services continued throughout His public ministry as well. At His trial before Caiaphas, Jesus declared, "I spoke openly to the world. I *always* taught in synagogues and in the temple, where the Jews always meet" (John 18:20).

So today Jesus invites each of us to find our place of service in the church where the combining of our gifts with fellow members will accomplish a hundred-fold more than if we were to go it alone.

Fourth, Jesus set an example in upholding the authority of the church and respect for its leaders. Someone is surely saying, "Hold it, my friend! That's a pretty severe stretch. I've read the gospels enough to know how Jesus lambasted church leaders. Calling people hypocrites and vipers doesn't sound much like respect to me!"

Perhaps those with that response stopped reading too soon. "Nevertheless even among the rulers many believed in Him, but because of the Pharisees they did not confess Him, lest they be put out of the synagogue" (John 12:42). We should not pass lightly over the fact that Jesus had friends among the church's leaders—friends like Nicodemus and Joseph of Arimathea, members of the Sanhedrin who didn't go along with the vote to have Jesus tortured and crucified. They were probably representative of many other lesser "rulers."

Was Jesus a Good Church Member?

And even the notorious "scribes and Pharisees" did not include the whole lot. In Acts 6:7 it says that "a great many of the priests were obedient to the faith." Where did these come from? Over the years those priests must have been there, sprinkled among the crowds that followed Him, listening and moving toward full acceptance of Him as the Messiah.

Now, it is true that Jesus denounced some church leaders for their hypocrisy, corruption, and abuse of sacred office. But we make a mistake if, in reading the cold black-and-white print, we supply our own tone to His voice. Ellen White says, "He fearlessly denounced hypocrisy, unbelief, and iniquity, but tears were in His voice as He uttered His scathing rebukes" (*The Desire of Ages*, p. 353). That is certainly much more apt to account for the fact that a great many of the priests believed.

In Matthew 23:2-3, Jesus said to His disciples, "The scribes and Pharisees sit in Moses' seat." That is, the authority to speak for God has been passed from Moses to them. "Therefore whatever they tell you to observe, that observe and do, but do not do according to their works; for they say, and do not do."

Again, He is saying, "I support church leadership when they teach the truth, even though their behavior fails to match what they teach. They sit in Moses seat. I ask you to show respect for their God-appointed position of leadership."

"He said nothing to unsettle their faith in the religion and institutions that had been committed to them through Moses. . . . He did not come to destroy confidence in His own instruction" (*The Desire of Ages*, p. 307). If that was His position with respect to the Old Testament church, it certainly must be equally true of the new church that He was, even then, in the process of building.

Fifth, Jesus encourages us, by precept and example, to support the church financially. Speaking of tithe, Jesus said to those in His day, "These you ought to have done" (Matthew 23:23). It would have been inconsistent for Him to say that if He Himself failed to pay tithe from His earnings as a carpenter or from donations given in support of His ministry. How could He commend the widow for giving her grocery money to a largely corrupt church if He didn't pay tithe according to His own instructions given through the prophet Malachi? He even sent Peter to catch a fish to pay a temple tax He didn't owe.

And finally, Jesus teaches us to stay by the church even when our fellow church members are faithless and backslidden. When Jesus organized His tiny church, He could well have wondered how it would fare after His departure. The envy, strife, and unlovely dispositions of His followers could have been most disheartening. But even *before* He left, He told them, "For where two or three are gathered together in My name, I am there in the midst of them" (Matthew 18:20).

In Revelation, He is pictured as walking among the lampstands that represent the church throughout its history. Talk about confidence in the future of the church! From the earliest moments of the New Testament church to the present, Jesus promises that He will not withhold His blessings from the *faithful* because of those who are *faith-less*.

Today, as the end-time church goes forth to engage the forces of hell in earth's final war, the issue is worship.

Discussion Questions:

1. Do your ideas about Jesus' relationship to the church need to change? In what ways?
2. How does the level of attendance affect the vitality of your congregation? Does your church have a program in place for involving those whose attendance is weak or nonexistent?
3. Is Jesus' teaching about the authority of the church generally accepted by the members of your church?
4. Have you ever thought of Jesus as a tithe-payer? Considering the spiritual condition of the church in His day, do we have an excuse to withhold our tithe because of the "badness" of the church?

Endnotes
1   See *The Desire of Ages,* 236.

Chapter Thirteen

THE ISSUE IS WORSHIP

"Give unto the Lord the glory due to His name; worship the Lord in the beauty of holiness" (Psalm 29:2).

To most Christians, including many Seventh-day Adventists, worship style is a non-issue. They consider it doctrinally fluid, something determined by personal taste and cultural values, not by any objective measure. To them, true worship is not defined by a particular genre of music, by dress, by conduct, or anything external. God is seen as being less particular than He once was. What really matters is that the worshiper has a feel-good experience.

There are churches today that advertise themselves as the "lighter side of church," "a fun place to bring the family." They claim their objective is "to create a church for people who don't like church." Now I'm in favor of making our worship services intensely interesting, but in these end times, I think preparing for Christ's return should fuel that interest, not a desire to be entertained. Our people need to be experiencing the kind of worship that will prepare them to remain loyal to God when the law is enacted that says, "As many as would not worship the image to the beast should be killed" (Revelation 13:15).

Seventh-day Adventists have schooled themselves to be watchful against any intrusions by religious or civil powers that might threaten their freedom to choose the day of worship. We tend to think of it almost exclusively as a Sabbath-Sunday issue, a *day* issue. The truth is, the *God* we worship, the *day* on which we worship, the *place* where we worship, and the *way* we worship are factors inextricably linked to each other, and all need to be receiving our close attention. All are sure to take on increasing significance in the end-time worship debate.

The prophetic picture is certainly clear. Seven times in Revelation 13 and 14 the word "worship" appears in connection with the life-and-death struggle between the beast and the remnant. To the bitter end, Satan will fight for a place on the throne occupied by God. In heaven he aspired to be "like the Most High" (Isaiah 14:14). In the wilderness of temptation, he was brazen enough to offer Jesus this world in exchange for a moment of worship. He is desperate to be worshiped as God.

We live in a society that has little regard for sacred things, and the virus is too easily caught. In Ezekiel 44:23, we read that God instructed the priests to "teach My people the difference between the holy and the unholy, and cause them to discern between the unclean and the clean." Modern Israel needs to learn the lesson as well. The forces that will fight the Battle of Armageddon are even now taking the field, and the issue around which the conflict rages is *worship*.

Let's review some of the basic elements that define the worship issue.

The *God* we worship is a holy God.

All the issues that revolve around worship center in the idea and image of God that we hold in our minds. That image must be shaped by the biblical portrait, not by one produced by a culture that tends to make God in its own image. "For the Lord is a great God, and a great King above all gods" (Psalm 95:3). No one can by searching find Him out (Job 11:7). He is our Creator (Genesis 1:27), Redeemer (Hebrews 9:12), Father (Matthew 6:9), Friend (John 15:14), and the Moral Governor of the universe (Revelation 19:16). He is holy (Isaiah 6:3), majestic (1 Chronicles 29:11), and eternal (Deuteronomy 33:27). He alone is worthy of worship (Exodus 34:14).

But of all the titles and appellations the Bible uses to describe God, "holiness" is the winner. Not love. Not mercy. Not faithfulness. *Holiness*. The six-winged beings seen by both Isaiah and John (Isaiah 6:3; Revelation 4:8) that serve in the immediate presence of God cry, "Holy, holy, holy is the Lord of hosts!" Holy is the Father. Holy is the Son. Holy is the Spirit. The call to worship Him is a call to holiness. "Oh, worship the Lord in the beauty of holiness" (Psalm 96:9)! "Be holy, for I am holy" (1 Peter 1:16). To be holy is to be Godlike. When we come to worship a holy God, it is assumed that it is our heart's desire to be made holy as He is holy.

Our secularized Christian culture does not resonate well with holiness. It prefers a God who is fun, a God who understands them, accepts them as they are, and leaves them as they are. They want a God they can worship with unveiled faces and rough-shod feet. "Thousands have a false conception of God and His attributes. They are as verily serving a false god as were the servants of Baal. Are we worshiping the true God as He is revealed in His Word, in Christ, in nature, or are we adoring some philosophical idol enshrined in His place?" (*The Faith I Live By*, p. 60).

We need to understand that all false worship is Satan worship. John makes precisely that point in Revelation 13:4: "They worshiped the dragon who gave authority to the beast." It is clear that whatever the visible object, person, institution, or false religious ideal being worshiped, Satan, the dragon, receives such worship as directed to him. If we really believed that, we would not rest day or night until we knew the difference between the true and the false.

We may smile at Isaiah's ironic poking of fun at those who carve out objects of worship from the same tree they use to cook their stew, but we, too, can be guilty of whittling out our own god—one adapted to our worldview and lifestyle more than by the Word. "God, for many, is what they want Him to be; admirable in proportion as He is useful for winning battles, assisting economic recovery, confounding the politics of the opposition, or crying [calling] up summer skies and happy days. . . This very broad-minded God, who is morally a little lax may be a

The Issue is Worship

soporific, but He is certainly no Saviour. . . . God is the best Master in the world, but He will be Master." [1]

The *day* on which we worship is a holy day.

God calls the Sabbath "My holy day" (Isaiah 58:13) and asks us to remember to keep it holy (Exodus 20:8). In Eden God sanctified the seventh day (Genesis 2:3). All that God had made up to that point was pronounced very good, but not holy. The six working days had produced nothing that was defiled, but they were not holy. Man was perfect, but not holy. The holy Sabbath was needed to make man holy.[2] "Surely My Sabbaths you shall keep, for it is a sign between Me and you throughout your generations, that you may know that I am the Lord who sanctifies you [makes you holy]" (Exodus 31:13).

We cannot separate our sanctification from a proper observance of the Sabbath. We need to covenant with friends, family, and church family to help each other keep the Sabbath. Will you and I stand up to the beast power and go to prison and to death in defense of a Sabbath we do not even keep? Not likely.

The *place* where we worship is holy.

We build houses of worship that include facilities not normally used for worship—foyer, furnace room, fellowship hall, classrooms, etc. All of these are dedicated to the service of God and should be treated with respect. But the sanctuary is the "most holy," as it were, a place dedicated solely to the worship of God. It is a place where we symbolically take the shoes off our feet. It is not a social club, a gymnasium, a theater, or a place of business. Human performance, human wisdom and cleverness, do not have the pre-eminence here. This is the place we come to worship the Most High God.

Those who choose to routinely and unnecessarily meet somewhere other than the house of worship where they hold membership could be making a serious mistake. Psalm 87:2 says, "The Lord loves the gates of Zion more than all the dwellings of Jacob." In these last days, to be found worshiping in the wrong *place* may be as displeasing to God as worshiping the wrong god on the wrong day and in the wrong way. It could be seen as worshiping in Mt. Gerizim when God is expecting us to show up in Jerusalem.

Of course the Lord loves to bless us when we meet with Him at the hour of morning and evening worship in our homes. But the psalmist says that He "loves the gates of Zion" even more. He loves to have us worship Him in the place where all of His people in a given area come together. The psalmist said, "I was glad when they said to me, 'Let us go into the house of the Lord'" (Psalm 122:1). We need to cultivate that attitude.

Holiness guides the *way* we worship.

This has become the battleground in many of our churches. I believe some of our members would give up the right *day* before they would give up *their way!* By *way* I mean all that happens under the heading of "worship service"—the preaching, the praying, the music, the announcements. If we come to worship a holy God in a holy place on a holy day, it follows that holiness will characterize all that happens next. Let's not forget that Satan seeks worship in the very place and from the very people where God is supposed to be worshiped.

Adventist worship should be different

Bible-based worship will be free of contradictions. There will be no clashing of worship styles; no conflict in the emotions elicited; no incompatibility between message and music. Worship will be reverent; common matters will be dismissed from our thoughts and conversation. It will be God-centered. We have come to listen to God and give Him our adoration and praise. There will be no praising and applauding of human performance.

Little defines a church more than its worship style. Worship in a Seventh-day Adventist church should be, in several ways, distinctly different. It constitutes a compact symbol of who we are. People who enter a Seventh-day

Adventist church for the first time have a right to expect something that sets it apart from the happy-clappy services found in other churches.

First of all, it is on a different day of the week. People not of our faith who join us for worship may associate Sabbath worship with the Old Testament, with law-keeping, and a special reverence for holy things. They may not yet agree with us about our choice of the day, but they sense that it encompasses something more than just observing Saturday in place of Sunday, and that "keeping the Sabbath day holy" must include especially reverent worship services.

Second, the fact that Adventists worship in the context of the earth's judgment hour should make a difference. "Fear God and give glory to Him, for the hour of His judgment has come; and worship Him who made heaven and earth" (Revelation 14:7). Adventist worship should not be dispirited or gloomy; rather, it should be characterized by a kind of solemn joy that grows out of implicit trust in a God who has them and their future in His hands. It should convey the impression that here are people who sense they are living on the edge of eternity—with all the excitement and sober reflection that engenders.

Third, Adventist worship is an act of loving obedience. It is coming into God's presence on the day and to the place of His choosing. It is worshiping God for the reasons He gives—to celebrate both His work of creation and redemption.

Fourth, Adventist worship will invariably make some reference to the Second Coming. This "blessed hope" should vitalize our worship with a constant infusion of expectancy. Jesus *is* coming again!

Holiness guides our choice of music.

We come now to the heart of the worship issue. The issue is worship, and nothing defines that issue like music. Nebuchadnezzar told the vast concourse gathered on the plain of Dura, "At the time you hear the sound of the horn, flute, harp, lyre, and psaltery, in symphony with all kinds of music . . . fall down and worship" (Daniel 3:15). One day soon, Babylon will again sound that call throughout the whole world—a call, not to the worship of a great golden image, but a call to join the fallen churches of Babylon in worshiping the Sunday god. It seems reasonable to believe that that call will also be accompanied by music. What kind of music would we expect that to be? Will it be uplifting and hymn-like? Or will it be that which is already familiar and attractive to billions of earth's inhabitants?

The place of the great hymns in our worship

I am not a musician and cannot speak to the subject in a technical sense. However, I feel compelled to point to a truth that I believe has been largely overlooked in the music debate. That is this: *God has given us the great hymns of the church as a safe guide to what is good music, and we ignore that gift at great peril.* Here are my reasons for making such a threatening statement.

1. The timing of the composition of the great body of Christian hymns is most significant. If one does even a cursory survey of when the hymns found in the *Seventh-day Adventist Church Hymnal* were written, it will be discovered that the great bulk of them were composed in the eighteenth and nineteenth centuries during a great spiritual awakening. The Holy Spirit was flooding the world with light. The prophecies of the books of Daniel and Revelation were revealing their secrets. The Spirit of Prophecy was being given to a teenage girl in the state of Maine. The Advent Movement was rising.

And Satan moved to counterwork the moving of the Holy Spirit. From time immemorial, he inspired the writing of secular and irreligious poetry. But when those Satan-inspired lyrics were set to music, the only music available was little different from that used by hymn writers. As the time for the giving of the three angels' messages approached, however, Satan began preparing other options. From Africa, via the slave trade, he imported new rhythms and improvisations into the American culture that would change the sound of music forever.

And of course God foresaw all of that. He foresaw the coming moral degradation of the twentieth century and the increasing difficulty His people would face in distinguishing between the sacred and secular in music. And He moved well in advance of Satan's corrupt stratagem to equip His people for what was coming. He did that by pouring out His Spirit on scores of hymn writers, giving His people a body of music that would serve as a wall of protection against the Satanic music soon to engulf the world. The *timing* here can hardly be viewed as accidental.

I readily acknowledge that some very good hymns have been written since the 1940s and 50s. But I don't think it can be denied that, when compared to the two hundred years before, there has been a remarkable decline in creativity and the composition of great hymns. It seems more than coincidental that the introduction of rock music and the abrupt decline of hymn writing have paralleled each other so strikingly in the modern era. 2. *I believe God gave us these hymns to define what sacred music is.* If sacred has meaning at all, it means there is a clear, recognizable distinction between it and secular music. We have the Bible as the great, unalterable benchmark for measuring ideas and behavior as they relate to the will of God. God saw that we also needed a standard by which to measure everything put forward by the composers of music. And again, I believe that standard is found in the great body of sacred music given to the Christian church. I believe the melodies of those hymns were created to imprint our minds with a sacred sound, so that *by sound alone*, we would have a way of differentiating between the sacred and the secular. People nurtured on such music know intuitively what sounds "hymn-like." People not so nurtured do not have that intuition, hence are ambivalent about any sacred/secular quality.

But when we diminish the place of the great Christian hymns in our worship services, we are defenseless

The Church That Does Not Fall

against the devil's substitutions. The line of distinction is confused, if not erased. We can tune back and forth from secular to religious stations not knowing when to dance and when to pray. Today a blind person would be hard-pressed to tell, by the sound of the music alone, whether he or she is in a church or a casino.[3]

We are told, even by some musicians, that the music is morally neutral, that one should not determine his church/casino location by the music alone,--that the words are supposed to do that. To me, that is like saying that reveille, the mother of all wake-up calls, and taps, the bugle call to signal the close of the day, could be easily switched. If that can be done, there is no such thing as "mood music."

The very expression "pop music" is another way of saying, "This is what sells." As Wolfgang Stefani has aptly observed: "If we have no external moral yardstick by which to evaluate our music, market forces will become the moral rudder by default. Ironically, within a Christian music context, this means that you end up with those knowing least about the Gospel determining most about its expression."[4] We need to hang on to the standard God gave us for making those distinctions.

3. These hymns were written with the worship of a holy God in mind, not as a vehicle for entertainment. One who was deeply involved in organizing upbeat worship services on a college campus denied the entertainment motive, saying that the students on her campus would "find it a hideous thought."[5] But that denial is easily tested today in churches where applause is considered an appropriate response. Performers with very little invested in musical training, but with a knack for mimicking secular pop artists, commonly get enthusiastic applause, if not a standing ovation. In the same service, the contribution of a serious musician who has spent years perfecting his or her skills on violin, harp, piano, etc., will commonly be greeted with barely-audible applause, if not with silence.

I'm not sure anyone today would even mildly object to the entertainment charge, much less categorize the idea as hideous. Large numbers of our people *know* it is entertainment and *want* it to be entertainment. Scores of Adventist "artists" have borrowed all the standard trappings of the entertainment industry and brought that image and style into the church. It fits what Ellen White called "a song, a frivolous ditty, fit for the dance hall" (*Testimonies for the Church*, vol. 1, 506). Any perceived uncleanness is purged away simply by calling it "contemporary Christian."

The great hymns call us to holy ground—to true, God-centered worship where the human shrinks to nothingness before the divine.

4. The quality of the lyrics in these hymns is worthy of the God we worship. Great hymns also qualify as great literature. Sacred music should not only sound sacred, the words should represent the very best in literary power and beauty of expression. The Psalms, so revered for their spirituality and poetic magnificence, served as the hymnbook for the Jewish temple services for centuries, and were the inspiration that guided the writers of many of our great hymns.

During the outpouring of the Holy Spirit and the Great Awakening referred to above, there seemed to be a spilling over of the divine influence into the whole world of art, literature, and music. The works of some of the literary notables of the time—Cowper, Wordsworth, Whittier, Newton, Watts, and others—not only began appearing in newspapers and literary journals, but also in hymnals. They were joined by scores of the lesser known whom God endowed with a gift of expression unparalleled in the history of the English language. Composers were likewise gifted to write music that fit the mood and message of the words. Church hymnals swelled with the new music, and it quickly became an integral part of the heart and soul of the Protestant Christian experience. Those hymns are still sung and appreciated today because they were made to last—the lyrics having a depth of content and the music an elevated style that is enduring.

By contrast, the lyrics of much (certainly not all) of the contemporary Christian music in vogue in our churches today are intellectually shallow and lacking in artistic beauty that is also attested by the fact that many are about as short lived as the pop music productions applauded one day and trashed the next by the general public.

Also, I find it ironic that the proponents of such music claim that we are supposed to tell the difference between the sacred and the secular by the words when the instrumental accompaniment is often so overpowering and the words so poorly enunciated that that is nearly impossible. If there is such an important message in the words, why do the composers/performers go to such great lengths to hide them? "The Holy Spirit never reveals itself in such methods, in such a bedlam of noise. This is an invention of Satan to cover up his ingenious methods for making of none effect the pure, sincere, elevating, ennobling, sanctifying truth for this time" (*Selected Messages*, bk. 2, p. 36).

5. *The great hymns of the Christian faith are characterized by harmony, not dissonance.* Psalm 92:1 and 3 says, "Sing praises to Your name . . . with *harmonious* sound." James McBride, a journalist and jazz musician, says this about rap music (also called hip hop) in an article for *National Geographic:* "I realize to my horror that rap—music seemingly without melody, sensibility, instruments, verse, or harmony, music with no beginning, end, or middle, music that doesn't even seem to be music—rules the world. . . . I live on a hip-hop planet."[6] The mystery is that McBride (or anyone) should even attempt to define such chaos as *music*.

The reader may protest that contemporary Christian music can hardly be compared to the above description of hip hop, and I agree. But while we're not there yet, I believe we're headed that direction. That prediction is supported by the fact that not long ago we would have found it impossible to believe we would ever embrace jazz and rock and their many hybrid forms to the extent we have. We may have chosen to take a road that has no turning. McBride's article carries this sub-heading: "All roads lead to hip hop in the evolution of African-American music."[7]

Ellen White uses words like "rich," "melodious," and "heavenly" to describe Christian music. She makes the rather blunt statement that *"noise* is not music" (*Evangelism*, p. 510). Does one need greater proof of her prophetic gift? She saw our day.

6. *The great hymns elevate the thoughts and create positive moods.* I think immediately of hymns like "Rejoice Ye Pure in Heart," "Joyful, Joyful, We Adore Thee," and "Come, Christians, Join to Sing." Hymns are often criticized as sounding like funeral dirges. The hymns just mentioned, and scores of others, debunk that denigration. There is far, far more variety in the tempo and mood of the great hymns than there is in jazz and rock. Some have a slower cadence calculated to allow the worshiper time to savor the beauty of the words and music; others are spirited and designed to create an excitement and desire for positive action.

Jazz, rap, blues, and rock, on the other hand, are absurdly monotonous. The only way for the listener to enjoy change is to switch from one genre to another. Far worse, such music is designed to cultivate sensual thoughts and feelings, or serve as an expression of discontent, even revenge. Do we really believe we can change the mood the music was *designed* to create by changing the words?

Alan Bloom, a widely read and respected university professor, says, "Rock gives children, on a silver platter, with all the public authority of the entertainment industry, everything their parents always used to tell them they had to wait for until they grew up and would understand later. Young people know that rock has the beat of sexual intercourse."[8] An aura of physical intimacy is prevalent in much of the so-called contemporary Christian music. The closed eyes, the breathy intonation, all appeal to carnal instincts.

Ellen White says sacred music "has power to subdue rude and uncultivated natures; power to quicken thought and to awaken sympathy, to promote harmony of action, and to banish the gloom and foreboding that destroy courage and weaken effort" (*Education*, pp. 167, 168). I think most students of her writings would agree that she would apply the above to all truly sacred music, with or without words.

7. *For the most part, the great hymns are doctrinally sound.* Why are these great hymns, so universally adopted by Protestant Christians, so free of doctrinal errors? Why is it that the composers did not seem to have a great burden to write about an eternally burning hell, baptism by sprinkling, salvation without obedience, or even Sunday sacredness?[9]

Here again is evidence of the Holy Spirit's intervention and guidance. The level of inspiration isn't the same, but just as we have a common Bible from which to learn the truth, we also have a common body of music from which to learn the truth. Obedience is taught in the song, "Trust and Obey," whether sung by Lutheran or Pentecostal. Baptism by immersion is taught by "The Cleansing Wave," whether sung by Episcopalian or Baptist. "Lo, He Comes" teaches the Second Coming to both Presbyterians and Adventists.

"There are few means more effective for fixing His [God's] words in the memory than repeating them in song. . . . It is one of the most effective means of impressing the heart with spiritual truth" (*Education*, p. 167, 168). The words of Christian hymns, as well as the words of the Bible, can serve to hold us on course when tempted to stray. Surely we can see that God was very much involved in producing music that would protect the church against the flood of corrupt music that would come pouring out of the devil's conservatory.

The Issue is Worship

So how did we get here?

How is it that music right out of the entertainment world came waltzing into our churches, music that is rightly associated with activities and lifestyles not favorable to godliness? And more particularly, how did it make such an apparently easy, unopposed entrance into a conservative, traditional-music denomination like the Seventh-day Adventist church?

We certainly did not arrive at our present near-universal acceptance of the big-beat contemporary music in our worship services as the result of a serious in-depth study of the Lord's counsel accompanied by much prayer. We got here because we sought direction from the gods of Ekron. We got here, in part, by copying the music of the mega-churches. We listened to pastors like the one who wrote: "We use the style of music the majority of people in our church listen to on the radio. They like bright, happy, cheerful music with a strong beat. Their ears are accustomed to music with a strong bass line and rhythm. For the first time in history, there exists a universal music style that can be heard in every country of the world. It's called contemporary pop/rock."[10]

We got here because we listened to a lot of fallacious reasoning. We were told that the notes and rhythm of music are themselves amoral—that only the words can have a spiritual dimension. We were told that music cannot be judged as right or wrong because music is cultural and a matter of personal preference. We were told that music is much too subjective to be reduced to a rational, objective values statement—a "doctrine" of music. We were told that our young people are turned off by old traditional hymns and would stop attending church if we didn't bring in the stuff they were used to getting on radio and TV. We were told that contemporary Christian music was the catalyst for rapid church growth.

And we bought into it. The sad fact is, even though some of us may be experiencing buyer's remorse, we are not asking the hard questions we should be asking, such as: Where are the churches that went from twenty members to mega-churches in a few short years? Where are the tens of thousands of consecrated youth who were brought in or kept in the church by the new music? Where are the hundreds of thousands of new converts, now active participants in the church, who were attracted to it by the irresistible spiritual power of "contemporary Christian music"?

We are victims of our own incremental compromise. We are in trouble today because we have for decades accommodated whatever was popular. Our ears have grown accustomed to the big beat, the dissonance, and shallowness of the world's music, and we have lost, or are losing, our taste for the truly sacred.

We would have spared ourselves decades of anguish, alienation, and split churches if we had simply followed the counsel of *The Church Manual:* "Great care should be exercised in the choice of music. Any melody partaking of the nature of jazz, rock, or related hybrid forms, or any language expressing foolish or trivial sentiments, will be shunned by persons of true culture. Let us use only good music in the home, in the social gathering, in the school, and in the church" (pp. 169, 170).

At this time in history, to abandon the great hymns of the church and permit them to be supplanted, even in part, by the devil's compositions is to face the enemy with swords of straw. These hymns are a crucial, God-given part of the Christian's defense against the forces of evil. We need to sing them now so we can join the angels in singing them in the future. Speaking of the saints ascent to heaven, Ellen White writes, "There are the columns of angels on either side; . . . then the angelic choir strike the note of victory and the angels in the two columns take up the song and the redeemed host join as though they had been singing the song on the earth, *and they have been.* Oh, what music! There is not an inharmonious note" (*Sons and Daughters of God*, p. 359).

The God we worship, the day we worship, the place we worship, and the way we worship—these are the end-time issues in the great controversy. We need to do all we

The Issue is Worship

can to make our churches models of true worship. By example, voice, and pen, we need to help our fellow worshippers see that "the hour is coming, and now is, when the true worshipers will worship the Father in spirit and in truth; for the Father is seeking such to worship Him" (John 4:23).

As we conclude, we'll look toward the future and what God has planned for His church.

Discussion Questions:

1. How can we, both as individuals and as a congregation, magnify the holiness of God without losing a sense of His love and sympathy for sinners?
2. How can we improve the reverence in our churches without our services becoming too stiff and formal?
3. Do you agree that the applauding of musical performances in our churches makes our worship services more like spectator events?
4. The main thesis of this chapter is that God has given us the great hymns of faith to keep us from falling prey to Satan's counterfeit music. Did you find this position defensible?
5. If you feel your church needs a seminar on what constitutes good music, would you know where to turn for help?

Endnotes

1 H. R. L. Sheppard, *Some of My Religion* (New York: Harper and Brothers, 1936), 110-111.
2 These thoughts taken from Andrew Murray, *The Believer's Secret of Holiness* (Minneapolis: Bethany House Publishers, 1984), 26.
3 Alan Bloom argues convincingly that "(music) is not only not reasonable, it is hostile to reason. Even when articulate speech is added, it is utterly subordinate to and determined by the music and the passions it expresses." *The Closing of the American Mind* (New York: Simon and Schuster, 1987), 71.
4 Wolfgang H.M. Stefani, "Is Music Morally Neutral?" *Here We Stand* (Hagerstown: Review and Herald Graphics,

2005), 408.
5   Ginger Ketting, "Crossways," *Adventist Review* (February 20, 1997).
6   James McBride, *National Geographic* (April 2007): 104.
7   *Ibid*, 111.
8   Alan Bloom, *The Closing of the American Mind* (New York: Simon and Schuster, 1987),73.
9   While it is true that hymns not doctrinally sound would naturally have been left out of the Adventist church hymnal, when I peruse hymnals used by other denominations, I find that they are more free of doctrinal errors than one might expect.
10 Rick Warren, *The Purpose Driven Church* (Grand Rapids: Zondervan, 1995), 285.

Chapter Fourteen

THE CHURCH THAT DOES NOT FALL

"On this Rock I will build My church, and the gates of Hades shall not prevail against it." (Matthew 16:18).

"Indeed I will make those of the synagogue of Satan . . . come and worship before your feet, and to know that I have loved you" (Revelation 3:9).

"Babylon the great is fallen, is fallen" (Revelation 18:2).

There is a church built by Jesus; there is a synagogue built by Satan. Against one, the armies of hell cannot prevail; against the other, the armies of heaven will prevail. One is a church that does not fail or fall; the other goes into oblivion.

John the Revelator gives us a good description of both. He foresaw the trials and triumphs of God's people in the end time. He saw 144,000 who "come out of great tribulation" (Revelation 7:14) and "follow the Lamb wherever He goes" (14:4). He identified the end-time church as "those who keep the commandments of God and the faith of Jesus" (14:12). He saw "those who have the victory over the beast, over his image and over his mark . . . standing on the sea of glass" (15:2).

John also foresaw that the churches of Babylon would crash and burn. He devotes at least three full chapters in the book of Revelation (17-19) to the woes of Babylon and her final demise. It is not a pretty picture. The kings and merchants weep and wail as they witness her collapse, while heaven is said to exult over her destruction because she has shed the blood of saints (Revelation 19:1, 2).

The Church That Does Not Fall

But what about now? Where are we in the course of the battle today? Let's look again at the statement that provided the impetus for this book: "The church may appear as about to fall, but it does not fall. It remains, while the sinners in Zion are sifted out—the chaff separated from the precious wheat. This is a terrible ordeal, but nevertheless it must take place" (*Selected Messages*, bk. 2, p. 380).

You may have wondered, as I have, what those words, "may appear as about to fall," could possibly mean. What makes it *appear* as if about to fall? Does it appear that way to you? If so, why? What signs and symptoms should we be looking for? How bad will things have to get before we decide it is "*about* to fall"? Some see it teetering on the brink of Niagara right now; others see it moving forward on solid ground. Let's look at a few examples of this "about-to-fall-but-does-not-fall" phenomenon.

Companies out, tribes in

Jesus said, "The love of many will grow cold" (Matthew 24:12); but He also said, "Many will come from the east and the west, and sit down with Abraham, Isaac, and Jacob in the kingdom of heaven" (Matthew 8:11). *Many* wax cold; *many* come. Ellen White says, "In vision I saw two armies in terrible conflict. One army was led by banners bearing the world's insignia; the other was led by the bloodstained banner of Prince Immanuel. Standard after standard was left to trail in the dust as company after company from the Lord's army joined the foe and tribe after tribe from the ranks of the enemy united with the commandment-keeping people of God" (*Testimonies for the Church*, vol. 8, p. 41).

Now as we stand on a hilltop watching the battle raging in the valley below, what is our assessment of how things are going? As we see the standard of the cross trailing in the dust and companies deserting from the Lord's side, we cry out, "Help! The church is falling!" But when we see *whole tribes* leaving the ranks of the enemy and coming over to the church's side, we say, "Praise God!

The Church That Does Not Fall

We're winning!" So if we focus on the thousands who are leaving, the church appears as "about to fall"; but if we look at the multitudes coming in, we decide that it will survive after all.

That prophecy is in remarkable fulfillment today. While many are leaving the church, in heart if not in body, particularly in the developed nations of the world, many more are joining the remnant in India, Africa, South and Central America, and elsewhere. Our personal perspective must constantly be informed by what's happening globally. If I am a member in a church of 200 but only 35 are showing up for Sabbath services, I am ready to vote for the "about-to-fall" verdict. But when I see churches in South America and India with memberships of 35 with 200 attending, my perspective shifts to the positive.

Separation and unity

"As trials thicken around us, both separation and unity will be seen in our ranks" (*Testimonies for the Church*, vol. 6, p. 400). It may not be readily apparent to many of our members, but today we are seeing a separation in our ranks never before seen in the history of the Adventist church. Thousands today choose their church home, not on the basis of proximity to their residence, but on the basis of lifestyle and worship style, thereby fulfilling the separation-unity prophecy. And from the perspective of those who would like to see the entire church firmly united on the platform of truth, this has certainly created an "about-to-fall" situation.

But we can be assured that the church triumphant, before it is dispersed to prisons and mountains, will continue to grow toward a level of unity never before known in its long history. When every worldly, compromising element has been purged—both by the preaching of the straight testimony and the threat of persecution—cultural, ethnic, and racial divides will disappear and all will give a clear and unified definition to the world of what it means to be a Seventh-day Adventist.

The Church That Does Not Fall

Bright lights go out

"Many a star that we have admired for its brilliance will then go out in darkness" (*Prophets and Kings*, p. 188), and no doubt the lamentation will be heard that the church is about to disintegrate for lack of leadership. But those "stars" will be quickly replaced. "The Lord will not allow His work to be hindered, even though the workmen may prove unworthy. God has men in reserve, prepared to meet the demand, that His work may be preserved from all contaminating influences" (*Ye Shall Receive Power*, p. 271). "He [God] will raise up from among the common people men and women to do His work, even as of old He called fishermen to be His disciples" (*Last Day Events*, p. 204). These prophecies are already being fulfilled in a remarkable way as thousands of laymen, many without formal theological training, are responding to the call to service around the world.

The threat of financial collapse

In our economically volatile world, we live with the momentary possibility that the church's financial structure could collapse like a house of cards. I seldom visit an Adventist church whose bulletin does not advertise a sizeable deficit in the monthly and yearly operating budgets. As attendance at our churches and schools in North America declines, pressure to keep operations in the black increases. Also, many are discovering that "liberal" does not necessarily mean "generous." The marginalizing of the faithful in some churches, causing them to seek fellowship elsewhere, is hurting those churches financially.

It seems likely that the closure of schools, hospitals, and other institutions—even local churches—could be a part of the future of the church. And that could lead all of us to conclude that the church is "about to fall." But I do not think such closures will be so widespread as to threaten the identity of the Seventh-day Adventist church. Here is a promise to support that conclusion: "The set time to favor Zion will soon come. God has provided men and means whereby His work shall be accomplished. He will not leave His people to shame, but will accomplish His work" (*This Day with God*, p. 193). The "means" spoken of here could very well come through sacrificial giving on an unprecedented scale by the faithful remnant. Houses and lands and savings may pour into the work faster than they can be spent.

We could multiply illustrations, but perhaps these will suffice. The present and future troubles that engulf the church are not to lead us to despair. Jesus says, "Now when these things begin to happen, look up and lift up your heads, because your redemption draws near" (Luke 21:28). God's servant says that when these difficulties come upon the church, "the half-hearted and hypocritical will waver and yield the faith; but the true Christian will stand firm as a rock, his faith stronger, his hope brighter, than in days of prosperity" (*The Great Controversy*, p. 602).

How does the true Christian do that? By developing the ability to see God at work in and through all these things, they see separation, but they also recognize a growing unity among the faithful. Can you see that? They see unworthy ministers, but they also see ministers faithfully proclaiming the full message of Bible Adventism. Do you know some of those, too? They see many becoming more and more deeply attached to the world, but they also see backsliders being converted. Surely you know some who have returned. They see many adding to their houses and furnishings and recreational toys; but they see others living frugally and giving generously to advance the gospel. There must be some of those in your church, too. They recognize that many have lost confidence in the Spirit of Prophecy, but they see others holding this treasure of truth ever closer to their hearts. How is it with you?

In other words, they see the power of divine intervention that continually turns "about-to-fall" into "does-not-fall." In a hundred ways, they see God acting to protect the church from destruction. They place their faith in God's promise that the church will not fall. They believe that the church that survived the alpha will also survive the omega. Here are some additional reasons for all of us to believe that, too.

The church that does not fall will experience a revival of primitive godliness. "Before the final visitation of God's judgments upon the earth, there will be, among the people of the Lord, such a revival of primitive godliness as has not been witnessed since apostolic times. The Spirit and power of God will be poured out upon His children" (*The Great Controversy*, p. 464).

The future is now. Such transformations are taking place in the lives of God's people at this very moment. "The Lord Jesus is making experiments on human hearts through the exhibition of His mercy and abundant grace. He is effecting transformations so amazing that Satan . . . stands viewing them as a fortress impregnable to his sophistries and delusions. They are to him an incomprehensible mystery. The angels of God . . . look on with astonishment and joy, that fallen men, once children of wrath, are through the training of Christ developing characters after the divine similitude, to be sons and daughters of God, to act an important part in the occupations and pleasures of heaven" (*Testimonies to Ministers and Gospel Workers*, p. 18).

Are you and I submitting our hearts to that kind of experimentation and experiencing that kind of transformation?

The church that does not fall comes through the shaking fully united and working with Holy Spirit power to finish the giving of the gospel to the world. "Servants of God, with their faces lighted up and shining with holy consecration, will hasten from place to place to proclaim the message from heaven. By thousands of voices, all over the earth, the warning will be given" (*The Great Controversy*, p. 612). "Servants of God," as used here, is not a description of pastors and evangelists alone; every member of the church is included.

We may find the thought discomforting, but the church that "does not fall" is a working church, driven by a love for the lost, and if we are to be counted as members, we must also be workers. "The truth is soon to triumph gloriously, and all who now choose to be laborers together with God will triumph with it" (*Testimonies for the Church*, vol. 9, p. 135).

Even twenty or thirty years ago, such prophecies still seemed far from fulfillment. We talked about it; we tried to imagine what it would be like when it did happen; but today we are seeing at least its beginnings. In addition to the regular employees of the church, there are "thousands of voices" being empowered by the Holy Spirit through Gospel Outreach, Adventist Frontier Missions, Adventist Laymen's Services and Industries, Maranatha Volunteers International, Amazing Facts, the Voice of Prophecy, 3ABN, the Quiet Hour, the Hope Channel—plus scores of lesser-known laymen's ministries. At the present rate of increase, the "thousands" predicted by Ellen White will soon swell to hundreds of thousands, if not millions.

The power of those voices will not reside in their numbers alone, but in the fact that they are *one voice*. "If Christians were to act in concert, moving forward as one, under the direction of one Power, for the accomplishment of one purpose, they would move the world" (*Testimonies for the Church*, vol. 9, p. 221).

I have always admired Ellen White's enthusiasm, which shines through words like the following: "In reviewing our past history, having traveled over every step of advance to our present standing, I can say, Praise God! As I see what God has wrought, I am filled with astonishment, and with confidence in Christ as leader. . . . We are now a strong people . . . We have everything to be thankful for" (*Testimonies to Ministers and Gospel Workers*, p. 31).

Ellen White wrote those words in 1902 when there were approximately 80,000 Seventh-day Adventists worldwide; now there are more than 16 million. In the same passage quoted above, she mentions the good work our colleges were doing. We then had four; we now have 106. She also expressed appreciation for our publishing houses. We then had two; we now have 65. In 1902 we had about 900 churches worldwide; we now have more than 120,000 churches and companies. Maranatha Volunteers alone has for years been building a new church every day on average. If Ellen White shouted "Praise the Lord!" for what God was doing in 1902, should not our shouts of praise be shaking the plaster loose in our churches today?

The church that does not fall will be composed of those who have an unusually fine-tuned sense of spiritual discernment. The devil's final assault on the church will be composed of an array of deceptions more clever, more closely aligned with the truth, than anything ever before experienced in the Christian world. Spiritualism will be used by Satan to lead multitudes astray.

We are susceptible to spiritualism's deceptions if we confine our definition to apparitions, Ouija boards, and séances. Ellen White dispelled that myth when she wrote: "Spiritualism asserts that men are unfallen demigods; that 'each mind will judge itself;' that 'true knowledge places men above all law;' that 'all sins committed are innocent;' for 'whatever is, is right,' and 'God doth not condemn'" (*Education*, pp. 227, 228).

Could it be that spiritualism is employing a whole new language today to disarm even the most wary? Do we hear its subtle voice in expressions like "contemplative prayer," "spiritual formation," "emergent church"? Could these words veil a misleading and hurtful message—the advocacy of an easy, cross-less, politically-correct religion?

The church that does not fall will be composed of those who have educated themselves to look beyond words and measure the worth of an idea or practice by the Word of God and the lives of the spokesmen.

The church that does not fall will be led in its final conflict against the gates of hell by consecrated Seventh-day Adventist youth. As one who has spent many years working with Adventist youth, my spirits are lifted when I see young people on the move for God. I received a shot of adrenaline not long ago when I read the following:

The Church That Does Not Fall

"There exists, today, an army of dedicated young people within the Seventh-day Adventist Church who yearn to demonstrate Nehemiah's leadership, Daniel's integrity, Mary's humility, Paul's passion for evangelism, and Christ's love for God and humanity."[1] That is not wishful thinking. Those words describe thousands of serious-minded youth who have joined the ranks of the Generation of Youth for Christ (GYC), a grassroots movement that is rapidly becoming a ground-swell for change in the Seventh-day Adventist church.

Of course not every dedicated Adventist youth has to be a part of GYC. The opportunities for all to have a part in a finished work are abundant. Belonging to a particular organization is not significant here; it is an attitude which is growing in young minds everywhere. They are making it clear that they are serious and committed. They are letting it be known that they are not afraid or ashamed of traditional music, godly relationships, modest dress, healthful living, and, above all, a passion for lost souls. These young people are saying the party is over. It's time to be thoroughly Adventist.

If this movement maintains its focus and vitality, it cannot help but move the church forward toward revival and reform. It could be the best evidence yet that the latter rain is about to be poured out. And it certainly may be the best of all evidence that the church that appears as if about to fall, will not fall.

The church that does not fall is composed of those who are finishers, not forsakers. When an airliner goes down, a ferry sinks, or some other tragedy suddenly takes the lives of our fellow human beings, we wait anxiously for the final report. Will it say that all survived? That a few were lost but that most survived? Or will we hear those despairing words: "There are no survivors."

Jesus said, "He who endures to the end will be saved" (Matthew 24:13). There will be survivors. Not as many as either God or we would like, but certainly thousands, and probably millions. The survivors are those still in their places after being forsaken by the majority. They are those whose faith survives the impersonation of Christ by Satan. They are those who will resist unimaginable pressure to worship the beast and his image.

And the Lord encourages them to hang on. "Brethren and sisters, look up; you who are tried, tempted, and discouraged, look up. Let no weary, halting, sin-oppressed soul become faint-hearted. The promises of God that come down along the lines to our times assure you that heaven can be reached if you will continue to climb. It is ever safe to look up; it is fatal to look down. If you look down, the earth reels and sways beneath you; nothing is sure. But heaven above you is calm and steady, and there is divine aid for every climber. The hand of the Infinite is reaching over the battlements of heaven to grasp yours in its strong embrace" (*Review and Herald*, February 17, 1885).

The church does not fall because the Bible prophesies triumph, not defeat. "But," someone says, "prophecy is conditional, and the church is not fulfilling the conditions." Apocalyptic prophecy is *not* conditional. The prophecies of Daniel and Revelation are considered by Bible scholars to be apocalyptic; that is, there are no conditions to their fulfillment other than those which God proposes to meet Himself.

For example, when God says that Greece will follow Medo-Persia in Daniel's lineup of world kingdoms, He does not say that *if* Medo-Persia will get its act together, it need never be replaced. He does not say that *if* Israel will repent and reform, the time allocated to them can be increased from 490 years to 1230 years. He does not say that *if* Laodicea fails there will be an eighth church. Apocalyptic prophecy is always fulfilled because it is a revelation of God's foreknowledge and His sovereign will. The human will does not control. God takes its fulfillment into His own hands and accepts full responsibility for meeting any conditions.

So when He says there will be a remnant who keeps all the commandments and have faith in Jesus, no human conditions or decisions can prevent its fulfillment. "The

The Church That Does Not Fall

program of coming events is in the hands of the Lord. The Majesty of heaven has the destiny of nations, as well as the concerns of His church, in His own charge" (*Testimonies for the Church*, vol. 5, p. 753).

When the gospel has been preached, when the final call has been sounded, when the last plague has been poured out, when the wrath of the devil has collided with the wrath of the Lamb, when the battle of Armageddon is over and the dust has settled, a voice is heard throughout the vastness of God's creation: "Here is the patience of the saints; here are those who keep the commandments of God, and the faith of Jesus" (Revelation 14:12). Here are the finishers! "The members of the church militant who have proved faithful will become the church triumphant" (*Evangelism*, p. 707).

The church does not fall because it is greatly loved and zealously guarded by the God who created it. This is the all-powerful, conclusive evidence that the church will not fall or fail. "The church, soon to enter upon her most severe conflict, will be the object most dear to God upon earth. . . . Will Christ, our representative and head, close His heart, or withdraw His hand, or falsify His promise? No; never, never" (*Testimonies to Ministers and Gospel Workers*, p. 20). "The church, enfeebled and defective, needing to be reproved, warned, and counseled, is the only object upon earth upon which Christ bestows His supreme regard" (*Testimonies to Ministers and Gospel Workers*, p. 49). "There is no need to doubt, to be fearful that the work will not succeed. God is at the head of the work, and he will set everything in order" ("Walk Not in Darkness," *Review and Herald*, September 20, 1892).

C. S. Lewis, in his *Screwtape Letters*, gives an imaginary account of how the devil and his agents work for the believer's destruction. One demon complains to the devil that a man assigned to him has recently joined the church. But the devil gives him this assurance: "There is no need to despair as long as this professed Christian does not see the church as we see her—spread out through all time and space and rooted in eternity, terrible as an army with banners. That, I confess, is a spectacle which should make all of us tremble."[2]

The devil, from his position wholly outside the church, may see the church in a truer light than many of its members do. We tend to see ourselves as weak, disunited, and riddled with apostasy. But the devil sees us in terms of our potential when filled with Holy Spirit power. He may laugh at the weakness of church members, but he has good reason to be intimidated by the church's Leader. He sees its past failures, but has sense enough to know by now that the Word of God does not fail, that the future triumph of the church is assured.

"We are almost home; we shall soon hear the voice of the Saviour richer than any music, saying, Your warfare is accomplished. Enter into the joy of thy Lord. Blessed, blessed benediction; I want to hear it from His immortal lips. I want to praise Him; I want to honor Him that sits on the throne. I want my voice to echo and re-echo through the courts of heaven. Will you be there?" (*In Heavenly Places*, p. 368).

Discussion Questions:

1. From your perspective, how is the church doing? Is it solid? Shaky? About to fall? What are the chief reasons for your assessment?
2. Again, as you see the church from where you are, what is most needed to bring in strength and stability?
3. How do you see the church in terms of its prophetic future? What can we expect to happen next?
4. Do you see evidence in your church that the youth are being prepared to join that "army" that will finish the work?
5. Are you able to look past those negatives that are a part of the "church militant" and focus on those things that describe the "church triumphant"?

The Church That Does Not Fall

Endnotes

1 Israel Ramos, "What Young People *Really* Want," *Here We Stand* (Hagerstown: Review and Herald Graphics, 2005), 61.
2 C. S. Lewis, *The Screwtape Letters* (New York: The Macmillan Company, 1942), 15.

We'd love to have you download our
catalog of titles we publish at:

www.TEACHServices.com

or write or email us your thoughts,
reactions, or criticism about this
or any other book we publish at:

TEACH Services, Inc.
254 Donovan Road
Brushton, New York 12916

info@TEACHServices.com

or you may call us at:
518/358-3494

www.ingramcontent.com/pod-product-compliance
Lightning Source LLC
Chambersburg PA
CBHW070538170426
43200CB00011B/2469